Advances in Entrepreneurial Economics and Sustainable Development - Volume 2

Digital Inclusiveness

Bridging the Divide in the Digital Economy

Advances in Entrepreneurial Economics and Sustainable Development

Series Editor: Elena G Popkova
(*Institute of Scientific Communications, Volgograd, Russia*)

Published:

Vol. 2 *Digital Inclusiveness: Bridging the Divide in the Digital Economy*
edited by Elena G Popkova

Vol. 1 *Climate-Smart Innovation: Social Entrepreneurship and Sustainable Development in the Environmental Economy*
edited by Elena G Popkova, Natalia G Vovchenko & Olga V Andreeva

Advances in Entrepreneurial Economics and Sustainable Development - Volume 2

Digital Inclusiveness

Bridging the Divide in the Digital Economy

editor

Elena G Popkova

Institute of Scientific Communications, Volgograd, Russia

World Scientific

NEW JERSEY • LONDON • SINGAPORE • BEIJING • SHANGHAI • HONG KONG • TAIPEI • CHENNAI • TOKYO

Published by

World Scientific Publishing Co. Pte. Ltd.
5 Toh Tuck Link, Singapore 596224
USA office: 27 Warren Street, Suite 401-402, Hackensack, NJ 07601
UK office: 57 Shelton Street, Covent Garden, London WC2H 9HE

Library of Congress Cataloging-in-Publication Data
Names: Popkova, Elena G., editor.
Title: Digital inclusiveness : bridging the divide in the digital economy /
editor, Elena G Popkova, Institute of Scientific Communications, Volgograd, Russia.
Description: New Jersey : World Scientific, [2025] | Series: Advances in entrepreneurial economics and sustainable development ; volume 2 | Includes bibliographical references and index.
Identifiers: LCCN 2024024453 | ISBN 9789811270819 (hardcover) |
ISBN 9789811270826 (ebook) | ISBN 9789811270833 (ebook other)
Subjects: LCSH: Information technology--Economic aspects. | Technological innovations--Economic aspects. | Entrepreneurship.
Classification: LCC HC79.I55 D548 2025 | DDC 303.48/33--dc23/eng/20240716
LC record available at https://lccn.loc.gov/2024024453

British Library Cataloguing-in-Publication Data
A catalogue record for this book is available from the British Library.

For any available supplementary material, please visit
https://www.worldscientific.com/worldscibooks/10.1142/13264#t=suppl

Desk Editors: Aanand Jayaraman/Geysilla Jean

Typeset by Stallion Press
Email: enquiries@stallionpress.com

https://doi.org/10.1142/9789811270826_fmatter

Preface

This book focuses on forming a systemic theoretical and methodological approach to overcoming the digital divide and the developing integrated practical recommendations to ensure digital inclusiveness through the tools of entrepreneurial economics. Its uniqueness lies in its revelation of a new perspective on achieving digital inclusiveness through the tools of entrepreneurial economics. The theoretical significance of the book and its contribution to the literature lie in the fact that this new perspective makes it possible to encompass all aspects of digital inclusiveness and formulate a systemic vision within entrepreneurial economics for the first time.

Of practical significance are the authors' recommendations of their innovative approach to addressing the digital divide based on the potential of entrepreneurial economics. The essence of the authors' approach is in revealing the potential of entrepreneurship to contribute to the fight against the digital divide in the interests of balancing and stabilizing the digital economy.

The first part of the book explains the technological provision of digital inclusiveness in entrepreneurial economics. The second part presents the social manifestations of the digital divide and governmental regulation of digital inclusiveness. The conclusion provides practical solutions to ensure the digital inclusiveness of today's entrepreneurial economics. This book provides its target audience of scholars studying the problem of the digital divide with a theoretical understanding of digital inclusiveness in connection with entrepreneurial economics.

https://doi.org/10.1142/9789811270826_fmatter

About the Editor

Elena G. Popkova, Doctor of Economics, is the Founder and President of the Institute of Scientific Communications (Volgograd, Russia), Professor at RUDN University (Moscow, Russia), and Director of the Laboratory of Scientometrics and International Rankings at Armenian State University of Economics (Yerevan, Armenia). She has authored more than 150 publications in Scopus (h-index 31), and edited more than 50 books and a large number of special issues of international peer-reviewed scientific journals. She is a member of the editorial board of the *International Journal of Economic Policy in Emerging Economies* and the *International Journal for Quality Research*. Dr. Popkova was the recipient of the 2020 Highly Commended Paper Award for the journal *On the Horizon* (Emerald) and has been named the Honored Worker of Science and High Technologies of the Russian Federation and Honored Professor of Osh State University (Osh, Kyrgyzstan). She was among the top 2% most-cited scholars of the world on Scopus in 2019–2021.

https://doi.org/10.1142/9789811270826_fmatter

Contents

https://doi.org/10.1142/9789811270826_fmatter

Introduction

The digital divide is a distinct manifestation of the social inequality characteristic of the digital economy. It has a complex nature. The technological aspect of the digital divide is related to the uneven distribution of advanced technologies in the socioeconomic environment. The geography of scientific and technological progress shows that it is predominantly led by major metropolises.

There are smart cities that lead within countries in terms of the penetration of digital technologies. Conversely, inhabitants of rural areas or remote regions distant from science and technology hubs encounter infrastructural barriers to accessing advanced technologies and face deficits and limited opportunities for their application.

The social aspect of the digital divide lies in the differential readiness of representatives from various social groups in embracing digital technologies based on two criteria. The first criterion is the susceptibility to innovation. Within the social sector, clear innovators actively support scientific and technological progress and eagerly acquire technical novelties. Some members of society are tolerant of scientific and technological progress. While they do not seek to be the first to adopt digital technologies, they are potentially open to their application. Conversely, there are clear opponents of scientific and technological progress who resist digital innovations.

The second criterion is the level of proficiency in digital knowledge and skills. Youth and individuals from socioeconomic categories with higher levels of education generally possess superior digital knowledge and skills. Other social groups typically exhibit gaps in digital knowledge and skills, along with difficulties in acquiring them due to time constraints. Even when willing, they often lack the readiness to apply digital technologies.

An economic manifestation of the digital divide is income inequality, which exacerbates the digital gap and, collectively, deepens social inequality. Advanced technologies typically have low affordability for the general population due to their high production costs and innovation premiums. Consequently, digital technologies undergo a cyclical transition. First, they circulate within the sharing economy as innovators resell outdated or worn-out technologies to representatives of other social groups. Second, in terms of pricing, the cream skimming pricing method is applied, wherein prices decrease as technologies become morally obsolete.

As for the ecological aspect of the digital divide, the development of the digital economy increases its energy consumption, leading to higher environmental costs of digital economic growth. Not all digital technologies can operate seamlessly and efficiently on clean energy. This has led to opposition from representatives of environmental communities against the proliferation of digital technologies. Therefore, significant differences in adopting digital technologies are observed depending on the degree of support for environmental values among social groups.

Bridging the digital divide means ensuring digital inclusiveness. Digital inclusiveness has many facets. Each facet of digital inclusiveness corresponds to a specific manifestation of the digital divide and explains the essence of overcoming this divide. One aspect of digital inclusiveness involves providing technological opportunities for digital modernization of the economy, which is achieved through overcoming the deficit of digital innovations and developing telecommunication infrastructure. E-commerce and its logistics contribute significantly to this because they make it possible to acquire digital technologies with a wide range of offerings on Internet marketplaces.

Another aspect of digital inclusiveness involves filling gaps in digital knowledge and skills, as well as overcoming moral and psychological barriers to the application of digital technologies. Continuous lifelong learning plays a crucial role in this, allowing individuals to tailor learning programs and implement them under flexible conditions, including through distance education platforms.

Another aspect of digital inclusiveness is the struggle against poverty, enabling the affordability of digital technologies for socioeconomic groups with low incomes. A promising solution in this case is the creation and development of public telecommunications infrastructure, through which all those willing can access digital technologies at low prices set by the state.

Another aspect of digital inclusiveness is the enhancement of the ecological sustainability of digital technologies, reducing resistance to the innovations of the digital economy from environmental communities. The enhancement of energy efficiency in digital technologies, endowing them with energy-saving properties and the capability to operate on clean energy, is of paramount importance.

The issue lies in the fact that the enumerated aspects of digital inclusiveness are mostly studied separately in the existing literature, hindering the formation of its comprehensive understanding. The uniqueness of this book lies in its rethinking of digital inclusiveness from the standpoint of entrepreneurial economics, which makes it possible to comprehensively cover all aspects of digital inclusiveness and form a systemic vision within entrepreneurial economics.

This book is unique in that it offers an innovative approach to addressing the digital divide, rooted in the potential of entrepreneurial economics. The essence of the author's approach lies in engaging entrepreneurship in addressing the digital divide. This approach ensures the balance and sustainability of the digital economy. Thus, entrepreneurship emerges as a unique force for uniting social groups and ensuring the stability of the digital economy.

In the technological aspect of digital inclusiveness, entrepreneurship can play a significant role in creating and developing public infrastructure. Digital technologies can serve as public goods provided by social entrepreneurship and public–private partnerships. In this case, support for digital inclusiveness serves as a manifestation of corporate social responsibility.

In the social aspect of digital inclusiveness, the contribution of entrepreneurship can lie in supporting lifelong learning. Concerning employees, enterprises can implement this through corporate training initiatives, while toward consumers, they can offer opportunities for free digital technology courses, thus addressing gaps in digital knowledge and skills among consumers. Therefore, providers of digital technologies can act as initiators in bridging these gaps.

In the economic aspect of digital inclusiveness, enterprises can provide digital technologies on preferential terms to low-income consumers. This can be achieved through special social programs supported by government financing. The socially significant directions for implementing such programs include the provision of digital technologies to schools, hospitals, and governmental institutions. Additionally, the prospective application of financing practices for consumers to acquire digital technologies is worth considering.

In the environmental aspect of digital inclusiveness, the role of entrepreneurship can involve maintaining close communication with representatives of environmental communities. Through these communications, it is advisable to allocate green investments toward developing eco-friendly digital technologies. Furthermore, based on these communications, enterprises should inform consumers and the wider public about improving the environmental properties of the offered digital technologies.

This book aims to develop a systemic theoretical and methodological approach to overcoming the digital divide and provide practical recommendations to ensure digital inclusiveness through the tools of entrepreneurial economics. This goal defined the design of this research and the logical sequence of presenting the results in this book.

The first part of the book describes the technological provision of digital inclusiveness in entrepreneurial economics. This provision encompasses inclusive management of digital personnel and the management of production–distribution processes in the entrepreneurship of the digital economy using advanced technologies such as artificial intelligence and machine learning.

The second part of the book is dedicated to the social manifestations of the digital divide and governmental regulation of digital inclusiveness. These manifestations encompass public infrastructure, the protection of human rights, and the enhancement of quality of life in the digital economy by addressing the digital divide.

This book concludes with the third part, in which prospective practical solutions for ensuring the digital inclusiveness of contemporary entrepreneurial economics are proposed and comprehensively presented. The authors' recommendations relate to the development of electronic democracy in the informational civil society and the personalization of goods and services across sectors of the digital economy.

The target audience of this book includes scholars studying the issue of the digital divide for whom this book will provide a theoretical understanding of digital inclusiveness in relation to entrepreneurial economics. Representatives of the academic community will also find the authors' scientific and methodological recommendations on managing digital inclusiveness in entrepreneurship within the book.

This book may also be of interest to stakeholders in the digital economy as it contains a detailed overview and discussion of international experiences in addressing the digital divide for enterprise representatives to peruse. Additionally, practical recommendations are also provided for using entrepreneurial tools to ensure digital inclusiveness.

Part 1

Technological Provision of Digital Inclusiveness in Entrepreneurial Economics

https://doi.org/10.1142/9789811270826_0001

Chapter 1

Prospects of Managing Digital Inclusiveness in the Entrepreneurial Economy to Support Sustainability

Elena G. Popkova

Armenian State University of Economics,
Yerevan, Armenia
elena.popkova@asue.am

Abstract: The research identifies the opportunities and advantages of managing digital inclusiveness in entrepreneurship. The research contributes to overcoming the digital divide in the digital economy. Through critical analysis, the research determines the applicability of the existing approach to managing social inclusiveness in the particular context of the digital economy and the potential for reducing the digital divide using this approach. As a result, the author identified serious shortcomings in the existing approach to managing social inclusiveness, which renders it inapplicable to combating the digital divide. The author developed a new approach to ensuring digital inclusiveness to address this issue. The distinguishing feature of the author's approach is that it relies not on the state, as in the existing approach, but on private entrepreneurship as the fight against the digital divide is carried out in the realm of the entrepreneurial economy. The wide-ranging opportunities and advantages of entrepreneurial management of digital inclusiveness to overcome the digital divide in the digital economy are substantiated by the high flexibility and effectiveness of this type of management . The theoretical significance of the author's conclusions lies in refining the specificity of combating the digital divide (i.e., achieving social inclusiveness in the context of the digital economy). The practical significance of the developed new approach lies in its ability to involve private entrepreneurship and thereby achieve more pronounced results in ensuring digital inclusiveness.

Keywords: Digital inclusiveness; digital divide; entrepreneurial economy; sustainable development; digital economy.

1. Introduction

The central idea of sustainable development and its goals (SDGs), as formulated by the UN [11] and involving a global marathon for their implementation, is to create a favorable socioeconomic environment for the lives of current and future generations, supporting progress in all its manifestations. One of the most important priorities on this path is constructing an inclusive society. This is explained by the fact that the social environment becomes favorable (open and friendly to everyone, providing freedom for economic activity) through inclusiveness.

The shift in technological paradigms associated with the transition to the digital economy has fundamentally changed the nature of the social environment of contemporary economic systems. Social inequality has taken on a new embodiment in the form of the digital divide. Moreover, the scientific and practical problem of ensuring digital inclusiveness as a result of overcoming the digital divide has become urgent. The existing approach to ensuring societal inclusiveness leads to restrained results regarding digital inclusiveness. Because of this, the problem of overcoming the digital divide remains unresolved, and this gap will persist and even deepen over time as the digital economy develops and global digital competition intensifies.

The novelty of this research lies in its reinterpretation of digital inclusiveness from the perspective of entrepreneurial economics. Thanks to this, the research presents an innovative vision of the prospects for ensuring the sustainable development of the digital economy through the provision of digital inclusiveness using the tools of entrepreneurial economics. The research aims to determine the possibilities and advantages of applying the instrumental apparatus of entrepreneurial economics to manage digital inclusiveness to overcome the digital divide in the digital economy.

2. Literature Review

The central scientific categories of the conducted research are as follows:

- Sustainable development of the digital economy in terms of the unfolding of its potential – enhancing digital competitiveness, accelerating the pace of digital economic growth, increasing exports of its products, and strengthening positions in global digital markets – with systemic support from SDGs [4];
- Digital divide in terms of differences in the availability and activity of using digital technologies among economic entities (social categories) and economic systems (territories) within the digital economy [1–2];
- Digital inclusiveness in terms of the result of combating the digital divide as a manifestation of social inequality and imbalance in the development of territories within the digital economy [6];
- Entrepreneurial economics in terms of economic activity carried out by entrepreneurship entities in the business environment under competitive conditions driven by market mechanisms [3,5,9].

The literature review allowed the author to outline the existing approach to inclusiveness management, which evolved before the transition to the digital economy. These outlines include, first, the basic assumption that the causes of inequality in the economic system have social and economic origins [8]. For example, income inequality arises from differences in the economic activity of economic entities, expressed in the varying amounts of income they receive.

Second, the key subject of inclusiveness management is the state. Ensuring inclusiveness is interpreted as a market failure overcome by government regulators [10]. Third, the toolkit for inclusiveness management includes (1) the development of values, the formation and strengthening of traditions of tolerance, and their integration into national culture;

and (2) the expansion of the range of social guarantees provided by the state to citizens [7].

However, the possibilities of applying the existing approach to managing digital inclusiveness to address the digital divide have not been sufficiently explored in the published literature. This creates uncertainty about how to manage digital inclusiveness. In particular, it is unknown what role entrepreneurial economics can play in this regard. This research seeks to fill the identified gap in the literature.

3. Materials and Methods

This research is conducted using the method of critical analysis. This method helps determine whether the existing approach to managing social inclusiveness is applicable in the specific context of the digital economy. Additionally, the author applies critical analysis to ascertain whether the reduction of the digital divide is possible with this approach. The critical analysis conducted revealed the following shortcomings of the existing approach to social inclusiveness management when applied to addressing the digital divide:

- The unreliability of the basic premise is that the causes of inequality in the economic system have social and economic origins. The causes of the digital divide have a technological nature. For example, the digital divide may be caused by differences in the availability of telecommunication infrastructure, advanced technical devices, or the level of proficiency in digital competencies.
- The government's ability to influence the integration of economic entities into scientific and technological progress is limited due to a lack of financial resources and insufficient flexibility.
- The toolkit for inclusiveness management is inefficient regarding the digital divide. Values and traditions are opposed to innovations embodied in scientific and technological progress. Social guarantees place a significant burden on the state budget but do not make it possible to keep pace with rapidly changing advanced technologies and digital devices and stimulate the acquisition of advanced digital competencies by the masses.

The identified shortcomings justify the inapplicability of the existing approach to managing social inclusiveness to address the digital divide.

4. Results

The entrepreneurial economy is distinguished by its enhanced flexibility, adaptability, and efficiency compared to state regulation of the economy. This defines the broad possibilities and preference for conducting digital inclusiveness management within the entrepreneurial economy. The author proposes the following comprehensive set of managerial tools for the entrepreneurial economy in addressing the digital divide.

The first tool is the development of digital competencies among employees through corporate training. Inclusive human resource management practices (HR practices) among digital personnel make it possible to transfer a significant portion of the risks of job automation to employers. Consequently, workers are much less susceptible to threats of downsizing or deterioration of working conditions and wages.

Expanded social guarantees from responsible employers are far more valuable to employees because they enable job retention, whereas state social guarantees are aimed at poverty alleviation and cannot guarantee employment in one's profession, let alone career advancement. Responsible HR practices enable workers to remain in their profession longer in the face of job automation through the continuous acquisition of new digital competencies, thereby enhancing their digital competitiveness in the labor market.

The second tool is the integration of SDGs into the practice of using digital technologies in entrepreneurship. Digital technologies are beneficial for sustainable development as they open new technological horizons for realizing SDGs. Widespread support for SDGs in entrepreneurship accelerates progress in their implementation. This also ensures inclusiveness in the digital economy by allowing all interested economic entities to participate.

The third tool is the provision of consumers with access to corporate smart technologies. Not every consumer can afford to acquire their own artificial intelligence, which hinders the spread of this technology in society. However, enterprises can acquire artificial intelligence not only for production but also for distributing their products.

Thus, enterprises can offer consumers the opportunity to freely use corporate artificial intelligence as a voice assistant and online consultant for selecting the enterprise's products, as well as a means of intelligent market analysis for multi-parameter comparison of products offered by different suppliers (competitors) in order to make more informed, rational decisions regarding purchases.

The fourth tool is the ethical use of digital technologies. Having invested significant capital in acquiring digital technologies, enterprises often seek to recoup their investments as quickly as possible. To achieve this, they extensively utilize digital technologies, which is not always ethical. For example, corporate machine vision may intrude upon the personal space of enterprise employees. Intrusive advertising and collecting personal information about consumers through tracking their search queries and purchases may violate the privacy boundaries of consumers.

The fifth tool is marketing support for the acquisition of cutting-edge technical devices by the general population. Different consumer groups (market segments) may be offered different conditions for purchasing enterprise products. For consumers who are more cautious about innovations, extended consultations on selecting technical devices, favorable conditions for using advanced telecommunication infrastructure, and personalized offers to enhance digital competencies may be provided.

The sixth tool is private investment in developing the digital economy to reduce the digital divide. Private investment projects can be directed towards the development of telecommunication infrastructure in remote areas and may involve conditions for preferential access to it for the least protected social categories of the population. Large enterprises can implement these projects individually and collectively, for example, based on clusters and public–private partnerships.

The developed toolkit for managing digital inclusiveness in the entrepreneurial economy is a promising way to overcome the digital divide in the digital economy.

5. Discussion

This research contributes to the literature by developing a new approach to ensuring digital inclusiveness. The specificity of the author's approach lies in the fact that, unlike the existing approach, it places emphasis not on the state but on private entrepreneurship as the battle against the digital divide occurs within the realm of the entrepreneurial economy. The distinctive features of the developed approach to ensuring digital inclusiveness are as follows.

First, in contrast to Sultanova *et al.* [8], the new approach adopts the basic premise that the causes of inequality in the economic system are not socio-economic but technological in nature. Second, unlike Tursunov *et al.* [10], there is no "market failure" in combating the digital divide; therefore, the key actor in inclusiveness management is not the state but private entrepreneurship. Third, unlike Sancino *et al.* [7], the toolkit for inclusiveness management involves not sociocultural measures of the state (development of values, traditions, and social guarantees for citizens) but marketing measures of private entrepreneurship.

6. Conclusion

Thus, the set goal has been achieved as a result of the conducted research. The author demonstrated the extensive potential and benefits of engaging enterprises in the management of digital inclusiveness to overcome the digital divide in the digital economy, thanks to the high flexibility and effectiveness of this approach. The developed new approach to ensuring digital inclusiveness involves the utilization of the entrepreneurial economic toolkit to address the digital divide.

The following managerial tools are recommended for use: (1) the development of digital competencies among employees based on corporate training; (2) the integration of Sustainable Development Goals (SDGs) into the practice of using digital technologies in entrepreneurship; (3) providing consumers with access to corporate smart technologies; (4) ethical use of digital technologies; (5) marketing support for the acquisition of advanced technical devices by the general population; and (6) private investments in the development of the digital economy to reduce the digital divide.

The theoretical significance of the author's conclusions lies in refining the specificity of combating the digital divide (i.e., achieving social inclusiveness in the context of the digital economy). The practical significance of the developed new approach lies in its ability to involve private entrepreneurship and thereby achieve more pronounced results in ensuring digital inclusiveness.

References

[1] Ali, K.S. and Faroque, A.R. Addressing the complexity of the digital divide and the role of government in addressing it: Role of government in bridging the digital divide. In: Islam, Q.T., Goel, R. and Singh, T. (eds.), *Fostering sustainable Businesses in Emerging Economies*. Leeds, UK: Emerald

Publishing Limited, pp. 127–145; 2023 December 4 [cited 2024 January 30]. DOI: 10.1108/978-1-80455-640-520231009.

[2] Hussain, H., Wen, J., Jiang, R., Waheed, J., Ali, W. and Khan, N.A. Analyzing the role of ICT in bridging the digital divide: A transitional analytical framework for ICT access to impact. *Library Hi Tech.* 2023 May 24 [cited 2024 January 30]. DOI: 10.1108/LHT-06-2021-0194.

[3] Litvinova, T.N., Khmeleva, G.A., Ermolina, L.V., Alferova, T.V. and Cheryomushkina, I.V. Scenarios of business development in the agricultural machinery market under conditions of international trade integration. *Contemporary Economics.* 10(4): 323–332; 2016 [cited 2024 January 30]. DOI: 10.5709/ce.1897-9254.219.

[4] Mkrtchyan, T.M., Tovmasyan, G.R. and Dallakyan, S.A. Sustainable development of the tourism sector of the Republic of Armenia in the context of an innovative economy. In: Popkova E.G. (ed.), *Smart Green Innovations in Industry 4.0.* Cham, Switzerland: Springer, pp. 383–391; 2023 December 8 [cited 2024 January 30]. DOI: 10.1007/978-3-031-45830-9_43.

[5] Osovtsev, V.A., Przhedetskaya, N.V. and Sagidullaeva, M.S. Conceptual model of adaptive management of strategic marketing: A system approach. *European Research Studies Journal.* 21(SI2): 666–677 2018 [cited 2024 January 30]; Available from: https://ersj.eu/journal/1293/download.

[6] Popkova, E.G., Bogoviz, A.V., Lobova, S.V. and Alekseev, A.N. "Underdevelopment whirlpools" as manifestation of disproportions of economic growth in modern Russia. In: Endovitsky, D. and Popkova, E. (eds.), *Management of Changes in Socio-economic Systems.* pp. 155–162; 2017 December 23 [cited 2024 January 30]. DOI: 10.1007/978-3-319-72613-7_14.

[7] Sancino, A., Scognamiglio, F., Corvo, L., Imperiale, F. and Pasi, G. Institutionalizing experimental places for inclusive social innovation: From utopias to heterotopias. *Voluntas.* 2023 June 12 [cited 2024 January 30]. DOI: 10.1007/s11266-023-00584-w.

[8] Sultanova, S., Zakirova, G. and Artikova, R. Assessment of the tax burden of the enterprise in the conditions of reforms in the tax legislation of the republic of Uzbekistan. *Journal of Critical Reviews.* 7(5): 282–285; 2020 [cited 2024 January 30]. DOI: 10.31838/jcr.07.05.51.

[9] Turginbayeva, A., Nurseitova, G., Zhakupbekova, G., Doszhanov, K. and Konysbay, A. Ability to use flexible project management in the hotel business. *E3S Web of Conferences.* 159: 04009; 2020 March 24 [cited 2024 January 30]. DOI: 10.1051/e3sconf/202015904009.

[10] Tursunov B.O., Uktamov, K.F. and Tukhtamuratova, A. Ways to ensure food security in the development of a digital economy. *Proceedings of the*

ICFNDS '22: The 6th International Conference on Future Networks & Distributed Systems. pp. 548–555; 2022 May 9 [cited 2024 January 30]. DOI: 10.1145/3584202.3584284.

[11] UN. The 17 Goals: Sustainable Development. [date unknown; cited 2024 January 30]. Available from: https://sdgs.un.org/goals.

https://doi.org/10.1142/9789811270826_0002

Chapter 2

The Inclusive Approach to HR Management

Mohichekhra T. Kurbonbekova[†,‖], Alexey V. Tolmachev[‡,], Sergey N. Patsyuk[*,§,††] and Sergey E. Akopov[¶,‡‡]**

[†]*Tashkent State University of Economics, Tashkent, Uzbekistan*

[‡]*Kuban State Agrarian University named after I.T. Trubilin, Krasnodar, Russia*

[§]*Sebryakovsky Branch of Volgograd State Technical University, Mikhaylovka, Russia*

[¶]*Rostov State University of Economics, Rostov-on-Don, Russia*

[‖]*m.kurbonbekova@tsue.uz*

[**]*tolmachalex@mail.ru*

[††]*snpa@mail.ru*

[‡‡]*Sergik-900@mail.ru*

Abstract: This research aims to develop an inclusive approach to HR management in the context of the digital economy. The experimental part of the research is conducted using the regression analysis method, which the authors employed to model the relationship between the

[*]Corresponding author.

features of employment inclusiveness and alternative HR management measures. The research is based on the advanced practices of the top 20 countries with the most inclusive employment in 2023. As a result of the modeling, the effect of each considered measure is quantitatively analyzed. The authors' conclusion is that the most promising measure of HR management is the development of digital skills among employees because this measure systemically enhances employment inclusiveness, increases labor productivity, and reduces the share of vulnerable employment. The authors identified the prospect of ensuring employment inclusiveness in developed and developing countries through improving HR management. The theoretical significance lies in the fact that the inclusive approach to HR management developed in the research allowed the authors to reevaluate this managerial practice in light of the new context of the digital economy and form a conceptual vision of the prospects for the systemic implementation of SDGs 8–10. The practical significance is expressed in the fact that the proposed recommendations for improving HR management practices in developed and developing countries will make it possible to fully realize their potential to ensure inclusive employment and will shape an inclusive global labor market by overcoming differences between these countries.

Keywords: Inclusive approach; HR management; inclusive employment; labor productivity; vulnerable employment; digital economy; digital skills of employees; corporate social responsibility.

1. Introduction

Human Resource Management (HRM) is one of those domains of contemporary organizational activity that proves most resistant to automation. This is because the workforce constitutes a social environment within the organization, where relationships, interactions, and connections cannot be fully translated into digital form, given the current capabilities of digital technologies.

Automation tools can only account for the external manifestations and outcomes of social communications, as well as the formal professional characteristics of employees. This is insufficient to transition HRM practices to the control of artificial intelligence. Therefore, even in the era of the digital economy, the practice of HRM in organizations remains within the purview of classical management.

However, this does not imply a complete absence of the influence of scientific and technological progress on this practice. For instance, the automation of production and distribution operations significantly alters labor processes and the composition of organizational personnel. This exacerbates the issue of ensuring inclusive employment. Examining this problem from the perspective of sustainable development goals (SDGs) is advisable because the goals serve as benchmarks for contemporary organizations and most accurately and succinctly formulate their priorities.

The Decade of Action challenges organizations to continue their course toward high-tech industrialization and implementing digital innovations supporting SDG 9. Simultaneously, within the framework of the discussed task, organizations need to improve employment conditions to support SDG 8, focusing on reducing inequality in workforces to support SDG 10.

In this context, developing an inclusive approach to HRM in the conditions of the digital economy is relevant because this approach represents a promising solution to the stated task, ensuring the systemic implementation of SDGs 8–10. It is worth noting that without deliberate effort, embodied in a distinct – inclusive – approach to HRM, employment inclusiveness remains unattainable in contemporary economic practice.

The reason is that high-tech industrialization and implementing digital innovations in organizational processes are pursued in the quest for maximum economic efficiency. In other words, organizations seek to enhance their marketing results, expressed in product sales and market share, and commercial successes, embodied in profits and profitability, with minimal financial and labor resources expenditures.

This implies tightening personnel policies, rigorous selection of the best human resources, and the creation of a social environment within the workforce marked by aggressive employee competition. Such an approach to HR management allows organizations to reap the aforementioned benefits but comes with significant costs for employees. Consequently, this approach is effective only in the medium term; in the long term, it is accompanied by destructive processes within the organization's human resources system.

The rupture of social ties among employees and the negative nature of their professional communications gradually lead to a disintegration of the workforce. As a result, in the long term, labor becomes individualized, and the formation of cohesive and productive work teams becomes impossible. Without teamwork, high-tech industrialization and integrating digital innovations into organizational processes are impeded.

Thus, a cycle of non-inclusive HR management closes, displacing the organization from the market. Breaking this cycle requires a transition to an alternative approach to HR management aimed at creating and maintaining an inclusive social environment within the organization's workforce. Balancing the interests of employees and employers is preferable in the long term because it ensures greater market success for the organization. In its endeavor to address the described problem, this research aims to develop an inclusive approach to HR management in the context of the digital economy.

2. Literature Review

This research relies on the concept of HR management as outlined in the publications of Kaushal *et al.* [5], Qamar *et al.* [9], and Xie *et al.* [14]. According to this concept, the indicators of employment inclusiveness are as follows:

- High labor productivity, indicative of healthy competition within the workforce [1,11];
- Protection of workers' rights, guaranteeing their long-term employment, and social and pension security, ensuring high employee loyalty to the organization or employer [6,8].

Although these indicators of employment inclusiveness have been reflected in a large number of published literature sources, the path to achieving inclusiveness in HR management in contemporary organizations remains unknown. This gap in the literature prompts the following research question (RQ): "How can employment inclusiveness, expressed in high labor productivity and protection of workers' rights, be achieved through HR management?"

Existing publications, such as those of Inshakova *et al.* [4] and Przhedetsky *et al.* [7], note that corporate social responsibility is the primary way to achieve inclusiveness within the workforce. However, this method emerged before the advent of the digital economy and did not fully leverage its technological potential in HR management practice.

Therefore, drawing on the works of Bogoviz *et al.* [2] and Samieva *et al.* [10], where the transition of all workers to the category of digital personnel (equal to each other and objectively evaluated in terms of professional competencies and work results) is considered a promising way to achieve inclusiveness within the workforce, this research advances the following hypothesis (H): The development of digital skills among workers makes it possible to achieve employment inclusiveness, expressed in high labor productivity and protection of workers' rights, through HR management. The economic significance of the proposed hypothesis lies in the formation of an impersonal workforce consisting of digital personnel, ensuring fairness and rationality in HR management. To test the hypothesis and address the RQ, this research identifies differences in the contribution of alternative HR management practices – corporate social responsibility and the development of digital skills among workers – to employment inclusiveness in terms of labor productivity and protection of workers' rights.

3. Materials and Methods

The experimental part of this research is conducted using the regression analysis method, which is employed to model the dependency of employment inclusiveness indicators – "GDP per person employed" (SE_1) as a measure of labor productivity according to the World Bank's assessment [12] and "vulnerable employment" (SE_2) as an indicator of workers' rights protection according to the World Bank's assessment [13] – on alternative HR management measures: "digital/technological skills" (HRM_1) as a measure of the development of workers' digital skills and "social responsibility" (HRM_2) as a measure of corporate social responsibility according to IMD's assessment [3].

The research uses the exemplary experience of the top 20 countries with the most inclusive employment in 2023. The sample includes ten developed and ten developing countries selected based on the criterion of the highest values of indicators reflecting employment inclusiveness according to World Bank statistics [12–13]. The temporal scope of the research is 2023. Earlier values are utilized for those indicators for which statistics for 2023 have not yet been calculated. The empirical basis of the research is reflected in Table 1.

Based on the results of the regression analysis, the HR management measure that contributes the most to employment inclusiveness is

Table 1. Signs of employment inclusiveness and HR management measures in the top 20 most inclusive countries in 2023.

Country name	Signs of employment inclusiveness: GDP per person employed, thousand dollars (constant 2017 PPP $)	Signs of employment inclusiveness: Vulnerable employment, total (% of total employment) (modeled ILO estimate)	HR management measures: Digital/ Technological skills, points 1–10	HR management measures: Social responsibility, points 1–10
Developed countries				
Austria	111.04	7.48	6.00	7.39
Bulgaria	58.25	7.02	6.31	4.90
Czech Republic	83.19	13.13	7.26	6.89
Denmark	117.87	5.26	8.41	7.98
France	106.46	7.69	6.94	6.13
Greece	81.14	24.45	6.28	5.35
Italy	111.32	16.03	6.33	5.75
Netherlands	109.88	12.29	8.35	6.87
Spain	92.83	11.14	6.73	5.80
Sweden	111.80	7.04	7.90	7.71
Developing countries				
Brazil	33.12	30.68	4.92	4.71
Colombia	35.13	47.57	5.69	5.63
Indonesia	25.83	49.35	6.89	7.33
Kazakhstan	55.96	20.66	5.78	6.58
Malaysia	57.81	20.92	7.12	5.74
Mongolia	32.80	45.88	6.00	4.56
Peru	24.81	52.60	5.48	5.51
Philippines	21.59	34.18	6.21	5.94
South Africa	47.31	10.47	5.59	5.54
Thailand	31.47	49.48	6.74	7.12

Source: Compiled by the authors based on IMD [3] and World Bank [12–13].

determined. The prospect of ensuring employment inclusiveness in developed and developing countries through the enhancement of HR management is identified. To achieve this, the maximum value of the chosen most effective HR management practice is substituted into the regression equations.

The authors compiled a forecast of changes in employment inclusiveness indicators for the Decade of Action (until 2030). Using trend analysis, the growth of indicators is determined according to the authors' forecast. Recommendations are proposed to unlock the potential of employment inclusiveness through the improvement of HR management separately in developed and developing countries.

4. Results

Based on the results of the regression analysis, two regression models have been derived to model the dependency of employment inclusiveness indicators on alternative HR management measures based on the exemplary experience of the top 20 countries with the most inclusive employment in 2023. The models are as follows:

$$SE_1 = -90.4080 + 21.3561HRM_1 + 2.9320*HRM_2. \quad (1)$$

Model (1) suggests that for every one-point increase in the development of workers' digital skills, labor productivity increases by \$21356.1. Similarly, for every one-point increase in the level of corporate social responsibility, labor productivity increases by \$2932.0. Therefore, the positive contribution of the development of workers' digital skills to employment inclusiveness exceeds that of corporate social responsibility by more than seven times.

The obtained coefficient of determination indicates that the considered HR management measures collectively increase labor productivity by 62.42%, demonstrating a close relationship between the following variables:

$$SE_2 = 73.3218 - 8.7117*HRM_1 + 1.1939*HRM_2. \quad (2)$$

Model (2) suggests that for every one-point increase in the development of workers' digital skills, the proportion of vulnerable employment decreases by 8.7117%. Conversely, for every one-point increase in the level of corporate social responsibility, the proportion of vulnerable employment increases by 1.1939%. Therefore, only the development of workers' digital skills contributes positively to employment inclusiveness; corporate social responsibility does not provide such a contribution.

The obtained coefficient of determination indicates that the considered HR management measures collectively increase workers' rights protection by 43.61%, indicating a close relationship between the variables. Thus, the HR management measure making the greatest contribution to employment inclusiveness is the development of workers' digital skills. Based on the regression analysis results, the prospect of ensuring employment inclusiveness in developed and developing countries through the improvement of HR management is identified.

To forecast changes in employment inclusiveness indicators for the Decade of Action (until 2030), the maximum value of the selected most effective HR management practice ($HRM_1 = 10$) is substituted into equations (1) and (2). The growth of indicators is determined using trend analysis based on the authors' forecast (Fig. 1).

To fully unlock the potential of employment inclusiveness in developed countries, it is proposed to enhance HR management by increasing the level of development of workers' digital skills by 41.82% (from

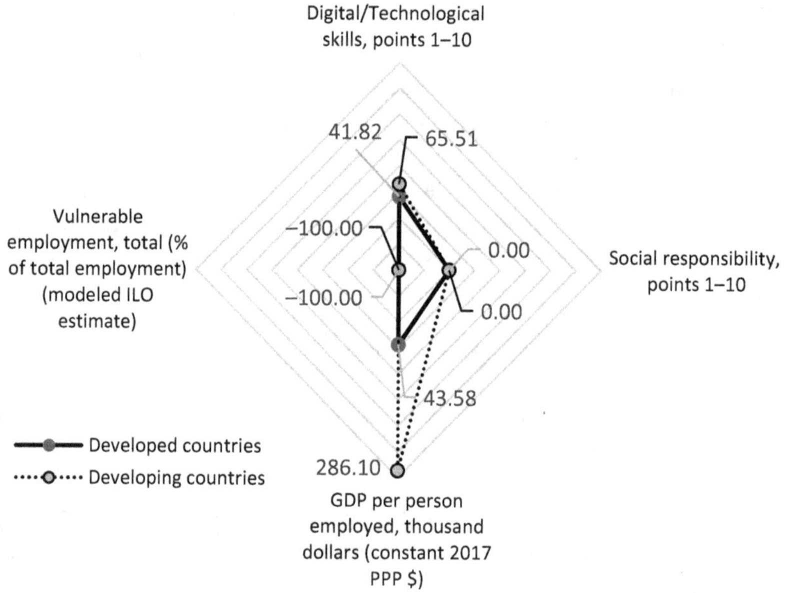

Fig. 1. Perspective on inclusive employment in developed and developing countries through improved HR management (%).

7.05 points in 2023 to 10.00 points by 2030). This enhancement will lead to the following advantages for employment inclusiveness:

- A 43.58% increase in labor productivity (from $98380 in 2023 to $141250 in constant prices by 2030).
- Achieving zero vulnerable employment compared to 11.15% in 2023.

In developing countries, it is proposed to improve HR management by increasing the level of development of workers' digital skills by 65.51% (from 6.04 points in 2023 to 10.00 points by 2030). This enhancement will result in the following advantages for employment inclusiveness:

- A 286.10% increase in labor productivity (from $36580 in 2023 to $141250 in constant prices by 2030).
- Achieving zero vulnerable employment compared to 36.18% in 2023.

Implementing these recommendations will foster an inclusive environment in employment sectors equally in developed and developing countries.

5. Discussion

This research contributes to the literature by advancing the concept of HR management and continuing a fruitful scholarly discourse, as observed in the works of Kaushal *et al.* [5], Qamar *et al.* [9], and Xie *et al.* [14]. The obtained results provide an answer to the posed research question. In contrast to the findings of Inshakova *et al.* [4] and Przhedetsky *et al.* [7], it is established that corporate social responsibility makes a modest and inconsistent contribution to employment inclusiveness, moderately increasing labor productivity and, instead of reducing, causing a rise in vulnerable employment among workers.

In alignment with the findings of Bogoviz *et al.* [2] and Samieva *et al.* [10], hypothesis H is substantiated, demonstrating that the development of workers' digital skills makes a substantial and consistent – exclusively positive – contribution to employment inclusiveness. This ensures significant growth in labor productivity and reduces the proportion of vulnerable employment. Therefore, developing workers' digital skills should form the cornerstone of an inclusive approach to HR management.

6. Conclusion

As a result of modeling the implementation experience of HR management measures in the top 20 countries with the most inclusive employment in 2023, the quantitative impact of each of the considered measures has been measured. The conclusion drawn is that the most promising measure of HR management is the development of digital skills among workers. This measure systemically enhances employment inclusiveness by increasing labor productivity and reducing the proportion of vulnerable employment.

The theoretical significance lies in the fact that the developed inclusive approach to HR management in the research made it possible to reevaluate this management practice in light of the new context of the digital economy. In this context, it also formed a conceptual vision for the systemic implementation of SDGs 8–10. The practical significance is expressed in the recommendations proposed for improving HR management practices in developed and developing countries. These recommendations will make it possible to fully realize their potential to ensure inclusive employment and global labor market by bridging the gaps between these countries.

References

[1] Ahn, D., Yoo, S. and Cho, S. Do competent managers increase labor productivity? Evidence from Korea. *Journal of Derivatives and Quantitative Studies*. 31(3): 242–260; 2023 July 6 [cited 2024 January 21]. DOI: 10.1108/JDQS-01-2023-0002.

[2] Bogoviz, A.V., Gimelshteyn, A.V., Shvakov, E.E., Maslova, E.V. and Kolosova, A.A. Digitalization of the Russian education system: Opportunities and perspectives. *Quality – Access to Success*. 19(S2): 27–32; 2018 July [cited 2024 January 21]. Available from: https://case.asu.ru/files/form_312-31738.pdf.

[3] IMD. World Competitiveness Online: Database. [date unknown; cited 2024 January 21]. Available from: https://worldcompetitiveness.imd.org/customsearchresults/criteriaresult.

[4] Inshakova, A.O., Sozinova, A.A. and Litvinova, T.N. Corporate fight against the COVID-19 risks based on technologies of industry 4.0 as a new direction of social responsibility. *Risks*. 9(12): 212; 2021 November 29 [cited 2024 January 21]. DOI: 10.3390/risks9120212.

[5] Kaushal, N., Kaurav, R.P.S., Sivathanu, B. and Kaushik, N. Artificial intelligence and HRM: Identifying future research Agenda using systematic literature review and bibliometric analysis. *Management Review Quarterly*. 73: 455–493; 2021 November 29 [cited 2024 January 21]. DOI: 10.1007/s11301-021-00249-2.

[6] Kersten, A., van Woerkom, M., Geuskens, G.A. and Blonk, R.W.B. Organisational policies and practices for the inclusion of vulnerable workers: A scoping review of the employer's perspective. *Journal of Occupational Rehabilitation*. 33: 245–266; 2022 September 9 [cited 2024 January 21]. DOI: 10.1007/s10926-022-10067-2.

[7] Przhedetsky, Y.V., Przhedetskaya, N.V., Przhedetskaya, V.Y., Bondarenko, V.A. and Borzenko, K.V. The role of social-ethical marketing and information and communication technologies in response to challenges of oncology. *European Research Studies Journal*. 21(SI1): 377–386; 2018 [cited 2024 January 21]. DOI: 10.35808/ersj/1188.

[8] Qalandarovna Abdurakhmanova, G, Jeong, J.Y., Rakhimjon Ugli Oqmullayev, R. and Utkir Ugli Karimov, M. The impact of tourism on employment and economic growth in Uzbekistan: An ARDL bounds testing approach. In: *Proceedings of the ICFNDS 2021: The 5th International Conference on Future Networks & Distributed Systems*. New York, NY: Association for Computing Machinery, pp. 431–439; 2021 [cited 2024 January 21]. DOI: 10.1145/3508072.3508158.

[9] Qamar, F., Afshan, G. and Rana S.A. Sustainable HRM and well-being: Systematic review and future research agenda. *Management Review Quarterly*. 2023 July 14 [cited 2024 January 21]. DOI: 10.1007/s11301-023-00360-6.

[10] Samieva, K.T., Saenko, I.I., Menshchikova, V.I. and Smetanin, A.S. ESG management of digital business using Big Data and Artificial Intelligence (AI) in support of the green economy in Russia and Central Asia. In: Popkova, E.G. and Sergi, B.S., (eds.), *ESG Management of the Development of the Green Economy in Central Asia*. Cham, Switzerland: Springer, pp. 3–11; 2023 [cited 2024 January 21]. DOI: 10.1007/978-3-031-46525-3_1.

[11] Tursunov, B. Provincial features of industrial production dynamics in the research of textile enterprises' financial security in Uzbekistan. In: Popkova, E.G. (ed.), *Imitation Market Modeling in Digital Economy: Game Theoretic Approaches*. Cham, Switzerland: Springer, pp. 601–610; 2022 [cited 2024 January 21]. DOI: 10.1007/978-3-030-93244-2_66.

[12] World Bank. GDP per person employed (constant 2017 PPP $). 2022 [cited 2024 January 21]. Available from: https://data.worldbank.org/indicator/SL.GDP.PCAP.EM.KD?view=chart/.

[13] World Bank. Vulnerable employment, total (% of total employment) (modeled ILO estimate). 2021 [cited 2024 January 21]. Available from: https://data.worldbank.org/indicator/SL.EMP.VULN.ZS?view=chart.

[14] Xie, J., Bhutta, Z.M, Li, D. and Andleeb, N. Green HRM practices for encouraging pro-environmental behavior among employees: The mediating influence of job satisfaction. *Environmental Science and Pollution Research.* 2023 September 9, 30: 103620–103639 [cited 2024 January 21]. DOI: 10.1007/s11356-023-29362-3.

https://doi.org/10.1142/9789811270826_0003

Chapter 3

AI and Machine Learning in Inclusive Development to Personalize User Experience and Increase Digital Literacy

Tatul M. Mkrtchyan[*,†,¶], **Aziza B. Karbekova**[‡,‖], **Dmitriy S. Zakharov**[§,**] and **Olesya K. Pakhomova**[§,††]

[†]*Armenian State University of Economics, Yerevan, Armenia*
[‡]*Jalal-Abad State University named after B. Osmonov, Jalal-Abad, Kyrgyzstan*
[§]*Sebryakovsky Branch of Volgograd State Technical University, Mikhaylovka, Russia*
[¶]*tatulmkrtchyan@yahoo.com*
[‖]*aziza-karbekova@mail.ru*
[**]*zakator@bk.ru*
[††]*pahomovaolesia@yandex.ru*

Abstract: This research aims to determine the prospects of personalizing consumer experience and enhancing the level of digital literacy in society through the utilization of artificial intelligence and machine learning in the practice of buying and selling goods and services. The research methodology is based on correlation and regression analysis.

[*]Corresponding author.

These methods are used to model the relationship between indicators characterizing the inclusiveness of the digital consumption society and the use of artificial intelligence and machine learning in the exchange of goods and services. Drawing on the international experience of the top 15 fastest-growing digital consumption societies in 2023 and IMD statistics, it is substantiated that the inclusiveness of the digital consumption society increases as the activity of using artificial intelligence and machine learning in the practice of buying and selling goods and services grows. The scientific novelty of the obtained results is explained by the fact that they have, for the first time, revealed the causal relationships between the use of artificial intelligence and machine learning in the practice of buying and selling goods and services and the inclusiveness of the digital consumption society. The authors revealed the potential for a wider application of artificial intelligence and machine learning in the trade of goods and services. Furthermore, they offered recommendations for realizing this potential. The practical significance of these recommendations lies in their ability to be employed within digital business strategies to increase sales and foster consumer loyalty. This will lead to increased availability of goods and services, reduced transaction costs, and increased efficiency in purchasing practices.

Keywords: Artificial intelligence; machine learning; inclusive development; personalization of consumer experience; digital literacy; digital consumption society.

1. Introduction

Contemporary socioeconomic systems can be termed digital consumption societies. This is elucidated by the fact that the social organization of these systems embodies a consumption society, wherein the values of individual consumption are promoted and the practice of artificially creating needs is widespread. The economic organization of these systems constitutes consumer capitalism, where the quality of life is determined by the volume of goods and services consumed and economic growth is rooted in the expansion of consumption.

The technological provision of socioeconomic systems entails the active utilization of digital technologies within them in production and consumption. For instance, digital technologies are employed to support the intelligent selection of goods and services and to consume electronic services (such as digital healthcare, e-commerce, and electronic governmental services). The issue lies in the fact that the pace of scientific and technological progress in the world significantly outpaces the rate of adaptation among the broader population. This poses two immediate threats to the development of a digital consumption society.

The first threat is associated with exacerbating the digital divide. Residents of large cities and holders of advanced digital skills and cutting-edge technologies (progressive youth, the wealthiest segments of the population) benefit from intelligent support in selecting goods and services and consuming electronic services. Meanwhile, residents of rural areas and consumers with a deficit in digital skills (elderly individuals and the poorest segments of the population) encounter increasing deficits and decreasing efficiency in satisfying their needs. Digital technologies have displaced pre-digital consumption practices, which have become less accessible and efficient.

The second threat constitutes the reduction in consumption rationality. Often, instead of stimulating more conscious choices of goods and services, digital technologies prompt impulsive purchases, which consumers later regret. Typically, this stems from low digital literacy. Even if a buyer possesses advanced digital knowledge (proficiency in digital technologies), insufficiently high levels of economic education hinder them from leveraging their knowledge and advanced technologies to their advantage.

To address the stated problem and neutralize the identified threats, this research proposes using artificial intelligence and machine learning for the inclusive development of the digital consumption society. The research objective is to determine the prospect of personalizing consumer experience and enhancing the level of digital literacy in society through the use of artificial intelligence and machine learning in the practice of buying and selling goods and services.

2. Literature Review

The theoretical foundation of this research is based on the concept of the digital consumption society formulated in the works of contemporary researchers, including Bogoviz *et al.* [1] and Gupta and Prusty [5]. The issues regarding the use of artificial intelligence and machine learning in the practice of buying and selling goods and services have been addressed in numerous published sources, including Ilina *et al.* [6], Samieva *et al.* [11], and Vanchukhina *et al.* [12]. However, the consequences of using the considered technologies for the inclusiveness of the digital consumption society are underexplored and not fully disclosed, which constitutes a gap in the literature.

Drawing on specific evidence of the shortcomings of artificial intelligence and the limitations of machine learning, some researchers [2–3] express the view that using these technologies in the practice of buying and selling goods and services reduces the inclusiveness of the digital society.

The rationale behind this viewpoint is linked to the fact that electronic data cannot encompass the entire spectrum of consumer needs or consider their psycho-emotional state. Thus, artificial intelligence cannot accurately assess and understand the buyer's needs. Consequently, artificial intelligence does not always provide accurate and sought-after assistance to consumers in making purchasing decisions.

In contrast, other authors [4,9–10] highlight that the psycho-emotional characteristics of the consumer, which are not easily quantifiable digitally, are the main reason for the irrationality of their purchasing behavior. Therefore, the abstraction of artificial intelligence from these characteristics enables it to provide consumers with the most objective and qualitative advice. In this regard, this research hypothesizes that the use of artificial intelligence and machine learning in the practice of buying and selling goods and services contributes to increasing the inclusiveness of the digital consumption society.

3. Materials and Methods

The stated objective is achieved through the pursuit of the following two tasks. The first task is to determine the impact that the use of artificial intelligence and machine learning in the practice of buying and selling goods and services has on the inclusiveness of the digital consumption society. To accomplish this task, the authors formed a sample from the top 15 fastest-growing digital consumption societies in 2023, selected based on the criterion of the highest values of the "household consumption expenditure – real growth, percentage change, based on constant prices" indicator (HCEG) as evaluated by IMD [7].

In this research, the "use of big data and analytics" (AIML) is employed as an indicator of the utilization of artificial intelligence and machine learning in the practice of buying and selling goods and services.

Additionally, the following indicators of the inclusiveness of the digital consumption society, apart from the aforementioned HCEG indicator, are used:

- "Digital/Technological skills" (DTSK) as a measure of digital literacy of the population, substantiated in the literature by Lybeck *et al.* [8].
- "Household consumption expenditure" (HCEX) as an indicator of personalization of consumer experience, substantiated in the literature by Wang *et al.* [13].
- "Customer satisfaction" (CMSF) as an indicator of personalization of consumer experience, substantiated in the literature by Zariman *et al.* [14].

Statistical data on the selected indicators are provided in Table 1. The correlation analysis method determines the relationship between the

Table 1. Use of artificial intelligence and inclusiveness in the top 15 fastest-growing digital consumer societies in 2023.

Country	Household consumption expenditure – real growth	Use of big data and analytics, scores 1–10	Digital/ Technological skills, scores 1–10	Household consumption expenditure (Percentage of GDP)	Customer satisfaction, scores 1–10
UAE	20.76	5.52	7.48	42.28	6.96
Turkey	19.70	4.73	6.20	57.53	6.67
Canada	18.06	6.14	7.49	52.75	7.29
India	15.61	5.98	7.28	60.55	6.65
Chile	13.14	4.67	7.00	63.86	5.90
Malaysia	11.31	5.43	7.12	57.60	7.27
Colombia	9.53	4.73	5.69	71.74	6.07
Argentina	9.45	4.58	5.64	63.68	5.29
Slovenia	9.15	5.12	7.00	54.19	6.99
Brazil	9.14	3.90	4.92	63.07	6.64
Philippines	8.29	5.16	6.21	75.94	6.92
Latvia	7.96	4.63	6.04	59.49	6.17
Greece	7.78	4.52	6.28	67.15	6.80
Iceland	7.56	6.21	8.12	52.21	7.85
Norway	6.83	6.39	7.33	32.41	6.82

Source: Compiled by the authors based on IMD materials [7].

studied indicators, while the regression analysis method shows how the inclusiveness of digital consumption society depend on the factor variable AIML.

The second task is to determine the prospects and develop scientific and practical recommendations to ensure inclusive development, personalize consumer experience, and increase digital literacy by improving the practice of using artificial intelligence and machine learning in the purchase and sale of goods and services. To achieve this task, the maximum possible value of the AIML indicator (10 points) is substituted into the obtained regression model and the expected change in the dependent variables is determined.

4. Results

To solve the first task and determine the impact that the use of artificial intelligence and machine learning in the practice of buying and selling goods and services has on the inclusiveness of the digital consumption society, the authors conducted correlation and regression analyses of the data from Table 1. As a result, four regression models were obtained. The first model reflects the dependency of household consumption expenditure growth on the activity of using artificial intelligence and machine learning in the practice of buying and selling goods and services:

$$\text{HCEG} = 6.06 + 1.07 * \text{AIML}. \tag{1}$$

Model (1) signifies that an increase in the activity of using artificial intelligence and machine learning in the practice of buying and selling goods and services by one point leads to a rise in household consumption expenditure by 1.07%. According to the results of the correlation analysis, the connection between the considered indicators is moderate – it is estimated at 16.92%. The second model reflects the dependency of the population's digital literacy on the activity of using artificial intelligence and machine learning in the practice of buying and selling goods and services:

$$\text{DTSK} = 1.33 + 1.03 * \text{AIML}. \tag{2}$$

Model (2) implies that an increase in the activity of using artificial intelligence and machine learning in the practice of buying and selling goods and services by one point results in an increase in the level of the population's digital literacy by 1.03 points. According to the results of the correlation analysis, the connection between the considered indicators is strong – it is estimated at 87.03%. The third model reflects the dependency of household consumption expenditure on the activity of using artificial intelligence and machine learning in the practice of buying and selling goods and services:

$$\text{HCEX} = 106.33 - 9.27 * \text{AIML}. \tag{3}$$

Model (3) implies that an increase in the activity of using artificial intelligence and machine learning in the practice of buying and selling goods and services by one point leads to a reduction in household consumption expenditure by 9.27% of GDP, thus rationalizing purchases. According to the results of the correlation analysis, the connection between the considered indicators is strong, estimated at 62.85%. The fourth model reflects the dependency of consumer satisfaction with purchases made on the activity of using artificial intelligence and machine learning in the practice of buying and selling goods and services:

$$\text{CMSF} = 4.04 + 0.51 * \text{AIML}. \tag{4}$$

Model (4) signifies that an increase in the activity of using artificial intelligence and machine learning in the practice of buying and selling goods and services by one point results in an increase in consumer satisfaction with purchases made by 0.51%. According to the results of the correlation analysis, the connection between the considered indicators is strong, estimated at 60.18%.

To address the second task and determine the prospect of inclusive development, personalization of consumer experience, and improvement of digital literacy through the expanded application of artificial intelligence and machine learning in buying and selling goods and services, the maximum possible value of the AIML indicator (10 points) was substituted into the obtained regression models (1)–(4).

As a result, it was established that due to the increased activity of using artificial intelligence and machine learning in buying and selling goods and services by 93.03% (compared to 5.18 points in 2023), the following benefits for the inclusiveness of digital consumption society would be achieved:

- An increase in household consumption expenditure by 44.49%.
- An increase in the level of digital literacy of the population by 50.29%.
- A reduction in household consumption expenditure by 76.66%, thus rationalizing purchases.
- An increase in consumer satisfaction with purchases made by 36.87%.

To put the identified perspective into practice, the following scientific and practical recommendations for improving the application of artificial intelligence and machine learning in buying and selling goods and services are developed and proposed for practical implementation:

- Expanding the range of personal settings for "smart" assistants and consultants.
- Introducing a procedure to assess the degree of consumer satisfaction with the results of intelligent decision support in making purchases (to improve machine learning).
- Creating customizable templates for decision support in making purchases by consumers to rationalize their shopping behavior (limiting expenses, prioritizing purchases, etc.).

Implementing the provided recommendations will ensure inclusive development, personalization of the consumer experience, and enhancement of digital literacy among the general population.

5. Discussion

The contribution of this research to the literature lies in refining the concept of the digital consumption society by unveiling previously unknown consequences of using artificial intelligence and machine learning in the practice of buying and selling goods and services for the inclusiveness of the digital consumption society. Unlike Bogoviz [2] and Bonetti *et al.* [3], this research argues that the use of artificial intelligence and machine learning in the practice of buying and selling goods and services does not reduce but rather enhances the inclusiveness of the digital consumption society.

In support of Dzhumanova *et al.* [4], Popkova *et al.* [9], and Przhedetskiy *et al.* [10], the research proves the proposed hypothesis; the advantages of using artificial intelligence and machine learning in the practice of buying and selling goods and services for personalizing the consumer experience and enhancing digital literacy are specified, including the following:

- Rationalization of purchases: accelerating the annual growth rate of consumption volume while reducing household consumption expenditure (in support of Wang *et al.* [13]).
- Increase in the level of digital literacy among the general population (in support of Lybeck *et al.* [8]).
- Enhancement of consumer satisfaction with purchases made (in support of Zariman *et al.* [14]).

6. Conclusion

Thus, the main conclusion of this research is that the inclusiveness of the digital consumption society increases as the use of artificial intelligence and machine learning in the practice of buying and selling goods and services grows. This conclusion is based on the international experience of the top 15 fastest-growing digital consumption societies in 2023.

The theoretical significance of the results obtained in the article is explained by the fact that they have revealed the causal relationships between the use of artificial intelligence and machine learning in the practice of buying and selling goods and services and the inclusiveness of the digital consumption society. The practical significance of the article is expressed in the perspective it discloses regarding the expansion of the application of artificial intelligence and machine learning in the buying and selling of goods and services, which can be utilized in digital business practices to stimulate sales and strengthen consumer loyalty.

The social significance of this study is justified by the fact that the practical recommendations proposed herein will contribute to increasing the inclusiveness of the digital consumption society by helping to bridge the digital divide and rationalize consumption (increasing satisfaction with needs while reducing expenses). This will enhance the quality of life by increasing the accessibility of goods and services, reducing transaction costs, and improving the efficiency of shopping practices.

References

[1] Bogoviz, A.V., Ragulina, Y.V., Komarova, A.V., Bolotin, A.V. and Lobova, S.V. Modernization of the approach to usage of region's budget resources

in the conditions of information economy development. *European Research Studies Journal*. 20(3): 570–577; 2017 [cited 2024 January 10]; Available from: https://ersj.eu/dmdocuments/2017-xx-3-b-53.pdf.

[2] Bogoviz, A.V. Perspective directions of state regulation of competition between human and artificial intellectual capital in Industry 4.0. *Journal of Intellectual Capital*. 21(4): 583–600; 2020 April 13 [cited 2024 January 10]. DOI: 10.1108/JIC-11-2019-0270.

[3] Bonetti, F., Montecchi, M., Plangger, K. and Schau, H.J. Practice co-evolution: Collaboratively embedding artificial intelligence in retail practices. *Journal of the Academy of Marketing Science*. 51: 867–888; 2022 August 19 [cited 2024 January 10]. DOI: 10.1007/s11747-022-00896-1.

[4] Dzhumanova, A.B, Kushakova, M.N. and Khodzhaeva, N.A. Formation of accounting management information in the control system of enterprises of JSC "Uzbekistan Railways." *International Journal of Advanced Science and Technology*. 28(14): 32–36; 2019.

[5] Gupta, S. and Prusty, S. Does consumer empowerment influence e-payment systems adoption? A digital consumer-centric perspective. *Journal of Financial Services Marketing*. 2023 June 26 [cited 2024 January 10]. DOI: 10.1057/s41264-023-00238-4.

[6] Ilina, I., Zharova, E., Turginbayeva, A., Agamirova, E. and Kamenskiy, A. Network platform of commercializing the results of R and D. *International Journal of Civil Engineering and Technology*. 10(1): 2647–2657; 2019.

[7] IMD. World Competitiveness Online: Database. [date unknown; cited 2024 January 10]. Available from: https://worldcompetitiveness.imd.org/custom-searchresults/criteriaresult.

[8] Lybeck, R., Koiranen, I. and Koivula, A. From digital divide to digital capital: the role of education and digital skills in social media participation. *Universal Access in the Information Society*. 2023 January 21 [cited 2024 January 10]. DOI: 10.1007/s10209-022-00961-0.

[9] Popkova, E.G., Litvinova, T.N., Karbekova, A.B. and Petrenko, Y. Ecological behaviour in the AI economy and its impact on biodiversity: Lessons from the COVID-19 pandemic and a post-COVID perspective. *Frontiers in Environmental Science*. 10: 975861; 2022 November 29 [cited 2024 January 10]. DOI: 10.3389/fenvs.2022.975861.

[10] Przhedetskiy, Yu, V., Przhedetskaya, N.V., Borzenko, K.V. and Bondarenko, V.A. Blockchain technologies in healthcare institutions: Focus on security and effective cooperation with the government. *International Journal of Economics and Business Administration*. 7: 92–99; 2019 [cited 2024 January 10]. DOI: 10.35808/ijeba/373.

[11] Samieva, K.T., Saenko, I.I., Menshchikova, V.I. and Smetanin, A.S. ESG management of digital business using Big Data and Artificial Intelligence (AI) in support of the green economy in Russia and Central Asia. In:

Popkova, E.G and Sergi, B.S. (eds.), *ESG Management of the Development of the Green Economy in Central Asia*. Cham, Switzerland: Springer; pp. 3–11: 2023 November 19 [cited 2024 January 10]. DOI: 10.1007/978-3-031-46525-3_1.

[12] Vanchukhina, L.I., Andronova, I.V., Sysoev, O.E. and Smetanina, A.I. The mechanism of innovative development of agribusiness based on AI, Big Data, and IoT for Transitioning to Expanded Reproduction in AgroTech. In: Popkova, E.G. and Sozinova, A.A. (eds.), *AgroTech: AI, Big Data, IoT*, Singapore: Springer; pp. 241–247; 2022 September 9 [cited 2024 January 10]. DOI: 10.1007/978-981-19-3555-8_25.

[13] Wang, C., Liu Y. and Zhou, H. Consumer consumption behavioral model for business intelligence using artificial intelligence. *Journal of the Knowledge Economy*. 2023 April 29 [cited 2024 January 10]. DOI: 10.1007/s13132-023-01391-w.

[14] Zariman, N.F.M., Humaidi, N. and Abd Rashid, M.H. Mobile commerce applications service quality in enhancing customer loyalty intention: Mediating role of customer satisfaction. *Journal of Financial Services Marketing*. 28: 649–663; 2023 November 4 [cited 2024 January 10]. DOI: 10.1057/s41264-022-00190-9.

https://doi.org/10.1142/9789811270826_0004

Chapter 4

Development, Accessibility, and Use of Technologies According to Inclusive Practices

Diana R. Galoyan[†,‖], **Aktam U. Burkhanov**[*,‡,**], **Ekaterina A. Zemlyacheva**[§,††] **and Fedor P. Potapov**[¶,‡‡]

[†]*Armenian State University of Economics, Yerevan, Armenia*
[‡]*Tashkent State University of Economics, Tashkent, Uzbekistan*
[§]*Volgograd State University, Volgograd, Russia*
[¶]*Sebryakovsky Branch of Volgograd State Technical University, Mikhaylovka, Russia*
[‖]*dianagaloyan@yahoo.com*
[**]*a.burkhanov@tsue.uz*
[††]*zemlyachevaekaterina@yandex.ru*
[‡‡]*efedrin.ru@yandex.ru*

Abstract: This research aims to determine the prospects for the development, accessibility, and use of technologies in accordance with inclusive practices. To achieve this, the authors examine the experiences of the

[*]Corresponding author.

world's top 20 leading knowledge societies and innovative economies as of 2022. Based on this international experience, the authors develop an economic–mathematical model that explains how the development, accessibility, and use of innovative technologies influence the inclusiveness of contemporary society. As a result, the authors conclude that research and development alone are insufficient for fully realizing the potential of ensuring social inclusiveness – achieving this requires the implementation of a comprehensive innovation management strategy, which also includes the development of ICT, technical and vocational education and training (TVET), and higher education. Using Russia as an example, the authors demonstrate that these measures of innovation management will enable the achievement of full social inclusiveness. The theoretical significance of the results obtained in the research lies in forming a conceptual understanding of the inclusiveness of knowledge societies and innovative economies. Specifically, this vision includes a clear prioritization of implementing innovation management practices. The practical significance lies in the forecasts compiled for a knowledge society and innovative economy in Russia, which elucidate the prospects for enhancing the practices of technology development, accessibility, and use in support of inclusiveness. Implementing the best perspective in practice will be facilitated by the newly developed approach to innovation management. A distinctive feature of the new approach is that it emphasizes the development of competencies in innovation use based on TVET and higher education, complemented by research and development and the growth of ICT.

Keywords: Technology development; accessibility of innovations; use of technology; inclusive practices; inclusiveness of Russian society; knowledge society; innovation economy.

1. Introduction

Inclusiveness embodies social justice and the openness of society to all its members; it is fundamental to the sustainable development of socioeconomic systems. While the concept of inclusiveness is singular and universal, its application to various economic practices has its specifics. For instance, the inclusiveness of the labor market implies the presence of effective social elevators, the inclusiveness of business requires a high level of market freedom and a favorable market environment, and the inclusiveness of a global market entails freedom in international trade.

From the perspective of inclusiveness, particular attention should be given to knowledge societies and innovative economies because they largely determine the state and prospects of contemporary economic systems. New technologies change everyday reality. However, these changes affect people's lives differently. To maintain social inclusiveness, technologies must, first and foremost, be useful and in demand in economic practice. This inclusiveness is necessary for technologies to receive significant and positive social feedback and sustain stable demand.

Second, technologies should be easy to learn and use. It is important for anyone interested to be able to acquire skills in the practical application of advanced technologies and use them easily when necessary. Third, they should be financially accessible – produced at a low cost and available at an affordable price. Fourth, they should be promoted in the market as technologies for mass use with corresponding marketing support, including advertising and distribution through widely accessible sales channels.

The problem lies in the fact that in today's reality, this is not always the case – not all advanced technologies meet the specified criteria. Many technologies are attractive only for their innovativeness, lacking valuable functional properties for consumers. Complex and rare knowledge and skills are required for their application or to derive benefits from their use. High production costs or high prices characterize most innovative technologies. They are positioned as elitist and distributed among narrow circles of consumers.

As a result, instead of supporting social inclusiveness, scientific and technical progress reduces it, deepening social stratification and exacerbating manifestations of social inequality. Recognizing the relevance of the problem at hand, this research aims to determine the prospects for the development, accessibility, and use of technologies in line with inclusive practices.

2. Literature Review

The theoretical foundation of this research is rooted in the concepts of the knowledge society and the innovative economy, defining innovation as the driving force behind the development of contemporary socioeconomic systems [8,11]. This research also draws from the work of Kitsai *et al.* [7] and Mulugeta Woldegiorgis [9] on the topic of social inclusiveness.

A literature review has revealed that, despite the abundance of publications, the consequences of scientific and technical progress for social inclusiveness remain insufficiently studied and unclear. The existing approach to innovation management, as outlined in the works of Ahmad *et al.* [1] and Cherif *et al.* [4], implies a focus on R&D. However, it is unknown to what extent this approach makes it possible to realize the potential for enhancing the social inclusiveness of contemporary society.

This constitutes a gap in the literature and poses a research question: "How do the development, accessibility, and use of technologies influence social inclusiveness?" Through content analysis of existing literature sources, innovation management practices have been systematized in terms of their alignment with the stages of the innovation process. The following practices were identified at the stage of developing innovative technologies:

- Conducting R&D [14].
- Development of advanced ICT [12].

The following practices were identified at the stage of dissemination (ensuring accessibility) of innovative technologies:

- Development of basic competencies in using advanced technologies based on technical and vocational education and training (TVET) [6].
- Development of advanced competencies in creating and using advanced technologies based on higher education [3].

The following practices were identified at the stage of implementation and use of innovative technologies:

- Creating a favorable economic environment for implementing and using innovations [2].
- Cultivating a culture that reduces social resistance to scientific and technical progress and encourages innovation [10].

In pursuit of an answer to the research question posed, the authors construct an econometric model of the systemic impact of the listed innovation management practices on social inclusiveness.

3. Materials and Methods

To understand how to align the development, accessibility, and use of innovative technologies with the inclusive practices of contemporary society, this research employs the regression analysis method. Using the chosen method, the authors conducted regression modeling to assess the regression dependency of social inclusiveness (measured by the social inclusiveness indicator calculated by GGGI [5] and denoted as SIncl) on the following set of innovation management factors (based on UNDP RBAS and MBRF statistics [13]):

- "Research, Development and Innovation" as an indicator of R&D activity, denoted as iv_1.
- "ICT" as an indicator of the intensity of advanced ICT development, denoted as iv_2.
- "TVET" as an indicator of the massiveness of basic competency development in using advanced technologies based on TVET, denoted as iv_3.
- "Higher Education" as an indicator of the success of advanced competency development in creating and using advanced technologies based on higher education, denoted as iv_4.
- "Economy" as an indicator of the favorability of the economic environment for the implementation and use of innovations, denoted as iv_5.
- "Enabling Environment" as an indicator of the level of cultural development in terms of reducing social resistance to scientific and technical progress and promoting innovations, denoted as iv_6.

The research sample includes the top 20 leading knowledge societies and innovative economies in the world as of 2022 based on the highest values of the SIncl indicator. The sample comprises ten developed and ten developing countries, ensuring its comprehensiveness (Table 1).

Based on the results of the regression analysis of the data in Table 1, the authors made two alternative projections of changes in the inclusiveness of Russian society. The first forecast assumes an isolated increase in R&D activity. The second forecast supplements this activity with other significant innovation management practices. In this case, the economic rationale of the forecast is to determine whether R&D alone is sufficient to realize the full potential of social inclusiveness or whether it requires a mix of innovation management measures.

Table 1. Inclusiveness and innovation governance in the world's top 20 leading knowledge societies and innovation economies in 2022, scores 1–100.

Country	Social inclusion	Research, development, and innovation	Information and communication technology (ICT)	Technical and vocational education and training (TVET)	Higher Education	Economy	Enabling environment
Developed countries							
Sweden	94.69	54.73	72.39	61.24	62.44	68.14	85.75
Switzerland	94.01	54.31	70.17	62.14	68.63	68.97	85.02
Austria	93.83	43.54	66.06	67.41	64.71	67.77	79.40
Netherlands	93.39	48.75	71.58	68.07	63.02	65.64	80.65
Norway	93.06	39.61	71.52	64.15	64.63	64.96	87.66
France	92.75	45.72	65.22	55.21	53.45	65.46	75.27
Germany	92.67	47.35	61.93	63.75	61.14	66.52	79.40
Spain	92.18	37.41	61.99	59.73	55.44	60.38	73.07
Finland	92.15	50.67	71.77	68.16	61.27	66.68	85.77
Belgium	91.52	43.71	59.80	64.90	63.14	67.62	77.96
Developing countries							
Belarus	88.25	28.20	52.80	58.92	49.39	46.69	51.63
Uruguay	82.09	25.14	53.35	53.40	47.81	50.51	79.56
Mexico	80.42	18.48	44.71	53.78	45.33	53.71	51.27
Mauritius	80.21	21.03	52.11	50.63	46.12	58.12	65.63
Kazakhstan	79.00	21.89	49.65	42.89	44.67	51.86	58.03
Chile	78.51	30.67	56.81	46.72	47.06	57.53	69.05
Trinidad and Tobago	78.42	18.04	50.74	44.94	51.11	54.79	55.00
Bolivia	78.24	27.25	38.69	62.58	52.16	41.48	50.48
Russia	78.14	27.35	50.98	52.41	41.10	49.71	48.10
Thailand	76.97	30.56	52.42	51.61	37.51	62.35	57.83

Source: Compiled by the authors based on GGGI [5] and UNDP RBAS and MBRF [13] materials.

4. Results

To determine how the development, accessibility, and use of innovative technologies affect the inclusiveness of contemporary society, the authors conducted a regression analysis of the data from Table 1. The results are shown in Table 2.

Table 2. Results of regression analysis.

Regression statistics						
Multiple *R*	0.9434					
R^2	0.8899					
Normalized R^2	0.8391					
Standard error	2.8325					
Observations	20					
Variance analysis						
	df	**SS**	**MS**	***F***	**Significance *F***	
Regression	6	843.2694	140.5449	17.5174	0.00002	
Residual	13	104.3013	8.0232			
Total	19	947.5707				
	Coefficients	**Standard error**	***t*-statistics**	***p*-value**	**Lower 95%**	**Upper 95%**
Y-intercept	43.3374	9.4026	4.6091	0.0005	23.0243	63.6504
iv_1	0.0642	0.1444	0.4443	0.6641	−0.2478	0.3761
iv_2	0.3384	0.1920	1.7621	0.1015	−0.0765	0.7532
iv_3	0.1925	0.1575	1.2220	0.2434	−0.1478	0.5329
iv_4	0.2668	0.1602	1.6650	0.1198	−0.0794	0.6130
iv_5	−0.0151	0.1653	−0.0913	0.9286	−0.3723	0.3421
iv_6	−0.0514	0.1146	−0.4479	0.6616	−0.2990	0.1963

In accordance with the results of the regression analysis from Table 2, differences of 94.34% in social inclusiveness among the studied countries are explained by variations in the impact of the considered set of innovation management factors on their social environment. This suggests a close relationship between the examined indicators, making it possible to construct a regression model depicting the dependency of social inclusiveness on the analyzed set of innovation management factors:

$$\begin{aligned} \text{SIncl} = {} & 43.3374 + 0.0642 * \text{iv}_1 + 0.3384 * \text{iv}_2 \\ & + 0.1925 * \text{iv}_3 + 0.2668 * \text{iv}_4 - 0.0151 * \text{iv}_5 - 0.0514 * \text{iv}_6. \quad (1) \end{aligned}$$

Model (1) indicates that the paramount importance of the inclusiveness of knowledge societies and innovative economies lies in innovation management during the stage of implementing and utilizing innovative technologies. For instance, with a one-point increase in the the prevalence of basic competencies in using advanced technologies based on TVET, social inclusiveness rises by 0.1925 points. Similarly, enhancing the effectiveness of developing advanced competencies in creating and using advanced technologies based on higher education by one point elevates social inclusiveness by 0.2668 points.

Second in significance are the innovation management factors during the development stage of innovative technologies. For instance, with a one-point increase in the intensity of developing advanced ICT, social inclusiveness rises by 0.3384 points.

Lastly, innovation management factors during the stage of implementing and utilizing innovative technologies, which also negatively impact social inclusiveness, rank the lowest in significance. For instance, with a one-point increase in the activity of government intervention in the sociocultural environment, social inclusiveness decreases by 0.0514 points.

The significance of $F = 0.00002$ and observed $F = 17.5174$. Thus, Fisher's F-test is passed at a significance level of 0.01, indicating the high quality and reliability of Model (1). Based on Model (1), the authors formulated two alternative forecasts for changes in social inclusiveness in Russia. The first forecast assumes an isolated escalation in R&D activity. In this scenario, the iv_1 indicator is assigned the maximum possible value (100 points, which is 265.63% higher than in 2022). In this case, the inclusiveness of Russian society only increases by 7.04% (from 78.14 points in 2022 to 83.64%).

The second forecast supplements this activity with other significant innovation management practices. According to it, the iv_1 indicator is assigned 100 points. There is also an increase in the intensity of developing advanced ICT by 46.86% (to 74.87 points compared to 50.98 points in 2022), an increase in the massiveness of developing basic competencies in using advanced technologies based on TVET by 27.17% (to 66.65 points compared to 52.41 points in 2022), and an enhancement in the effectiveness of developing advanced competencies in creating and using advanced technologies based on higher education by 40.19% (to 57.62 points compared to 41.10 points in 2022).

This makes it possible to achieve full social inclusiveness in Russian society (100 points, +27.98% compared to 2022). Based on the results of the regression analysis and the formulated forecasts, the authors proposed a new approach to innovation management in which R&D activities, while significant, are not the main practice of innovation management. In the proposed approach, key practices are the development of competencies in using innovations based on TVET and higher education. Conducting R&D activities and developing ICT complement them.

5. Discussion

This research contributes to the literature by filling gaps in scientific knowledge at the intersection of the concepts of the knowledge society and the innovation economy (continuing the series of works by Lobova *et al.* [8] and Pricopoaia *et al.* [11]), as well as the concept of social inclusiveness (continuing the series of works by Kitsai *et al.* [7] and Mulugeta Woldegiorgis [9]).

In contrast to Przhedetsky *et al.* [12] and Zhao *et al.* [14], the authors found that the practices of innovation management implemented during the development stage of innovative technologies have a secondary, rather than primary, significance for achieving social inclusiveness. Unlike Carabregu-Vokshi *et al.* [3] and Jumambayev *et al.* [6], it is identified that the practices of innovation management implemented during the dissemination stage (ensuring accessibility) of innovative technologies are crucial for ensuring social inclusiveness. In contrast to Bogoviz *et al.* [2] and Popkova *et al.* [10], the authors demonstrated that the practices of innovation management implemented during the implementation and utilization stage of innovative technologies do not contribute to social inclusiveness.

In contrast to Ahmad *et al.* [1] and Cherif *et al.* [4], the authors substantiated that the approach to innovation management should not focus efforts solely on conducting R&D activities but should involve the systemic implementation of interconnected innovation management practices, with the core being the development of creative and technical competencies through TVET and higher education, complemented by the development of ICT.

6. Conclusion

The conclusions of this research emphasize that mere R&D activities are insufficient for fully unleashing the potential to ensure social inclusiveness. It requires implementing a comprehensive innovation management framework encompassing the development of ICT, TVET, and higher education. Using Russia as an example, the authors demonstrated that these innovation management measures can lead to complete social inclusiveness.

The theoretical significance of the research findings lies in shaping a conceptual understanding of social inclusiveness within the knowledge society and the innovation economy. This vision notably includes a clear prioritization when implementing innovation management practices.

In practical terms, the significance lies in the forecasts crafted for the Russian knowledge society and innovation economy, elucidating the prospects for enhancing practices in technology development, accessibility, and utilization to support inclusiveness. Implementing the best perspective in practice will be facilitated by the newly developed approach to innovation management.

References

[1] Ahmad, M., Haq, Z.U., Iqbal, J. and Khan, Sh. Dating the business cycles: Research and Development (R&D) expenditures and new knowledge creation in OECD economies over the business cycles. *Journal of the Knowledge Economy*. 14: 3929–3973; 2023 April 13 [cited 2024 January 11]. DOI: 10.1007/s13132-022-01018-6.

[2] Bogoviz, A.V., Sandu, I.S., Demishkevich, G.M. and Ryzhenkova, N.E. Economic aspects of formation of organizational and economic mechanism of the innovational infrastructure of the EAEU countries' agro-industrial complex. In: Popkova, E. and Ostrovskaya, V. (eds.), *Perspectives on the Use of New Information and Communication Technology (ICT) In the Modern Economy*. Cham, Switzerland: Springer; pp. 108–117; 2018 June 5 [cited 2024 January 11]. DOI: 10.1007/978-3-319-90835-9_13.

[3] Carabregu-Vokshi, M., Ogruk-Maz, G., Yildirim, S., Dedaj, B. and Zeqiri, A. 21st century digital skills of higher education students during COVID-19 – is it possible to enhance digital skills of higher education students through E-Learning? *Education and Information Technologies*. 29: 103–137; 2023 November 3 [cited 2024 January 11]. DOI: 10.1007/s10639-023-12232-3.

[4] Cherif, R., Grimpe, C., Hasanov, F. and Sofka, W. Promoting innovation: The differential impact of R&D subsidies. *Journal of Industry, Competition and Trade*. 23: 187–241; 2023 September 18 [cited 2024 January 11]. DOI: 10.1007/s10842-023-00400-7.

[5] Global Green Growth Institute (GGGI). Global Green Growth Index 2022: Measuring performance in achieving SDG targets. 2022 December [cited 2024 January 11]. Available from: https://greengrowthindex.gggi.org/wp-content/uploads/2023/02/2022-Green-Growth-Index-1.pdf.

[6] Jumambayev, S., Turginbayeva, A. and Moldabekova, A. The impact of new technologies on employment in Kazakhstan. *Proceedings of the IBIMA 2018: 32nd International Business Information Management Association Conference – Vision 2020: Sustainable Economic Development and Application of Innovation Management from Regional Expansion to Global growth.* pp. 2184–2188; Seville, Spain: IBIMA; 2018.

[7] Kitsai, J.A., Karpushova, S.E., Petrenko, E.S. and Smetanina, A.I. Social entrepreneurship as an institute of sustainable development risk management. In: Popkova, E.G. (eds.), *Sustainable Development Risks and Risk Management* [Internet]. Cham, Switzerland: Springer; pp. 363–367; 2023 October 19 [cited 2024 January 11]. DOI: 10.1007/978-3-031-34256-1_63.

[8] Lobova, S.V., Alekseev, A.N., Litvinova, T.N. and Sadovnikova, N.A. Labor division and advantages and limits of participation in creation of intangible assets in industry 4.0: humans versus machines. *Journal of Intellectual Capital.* 21(4): 623–638; 2020 April 15 [cited 2024 January 11]. DOI: 10.1108/JIC-11-2019-0277.

[9] Mulugeta, Woldegiorgis, M. Inequality, social protection policy, and inclusion: pertinent theories and empirical evidence. *Journal of Social and Economic Development.* 24: 241–265; 2022 May 11 [cited 2024 January 11]. DOI: 10.1007/s40847-022-00185-1.

[10] Popkova, E.G., Bogoviz, A.V. and Lobova, S.V. Vacuum in the structure of human capital: A view from the position of the theory of vacuum. In: *Human Capital: Perspectives, Challenges and Future Directions.* Hauppauge, NY: Nova Science Publishers; pp. 163–181; 2017.

[11] Pricopoaia, O., Busila, A.V., Cristache, N., Susanu, I. and Matis, C. Challenges for entrepreneurial innovation: Startups as tools for a better knowledge-based economy. *International Entrepreneurship and Management Journal.* 2023 November 18 [cited 2024 January 11]. DOI: 10.1007/s11365-023-00923-9.

[12] Przhedetsky, Y.V., Przhedetskaya, N.V., Przhedetskaya, V.Y., Bondarenko, V.A. and Borzenko, K.V. The role of social-ethical marketing and information and communication technologies in response to challenges of oncology. *European Research Studies Journal.* 21(SI1): 377–386; 2018 [cited 2024 January 11]. DOI: 10.35808/ersj/1188.

[13] United Nations Development Programme's Regional Bureau for Arab States (UNDP RBAS) and Mohammed Bin Rashid Al Maktoum Knowledge Foundation (MBRF). Global Knowledge Index 2022. [date unknown; cited 2024 January 11]. Available from: https://www.knowledge4all.com/ranking.

[14] Zhao, Q., Lee, B.H., Luo, J. and Chen, H. R&D internationalization and innovation performance: The impact of executives' characteristics. *Journal of the Knowledge Economy.* 2023 June 9 [cited 2024 January 11]. DOI: 10.1007/s13132-023-01418-2.

https://doi.org/10.1142/9789811270826_0005

Chapter 5

Digital Inclusiveness in Entrepreneurship Through the Lens of the Technological Barriers of Markets

Aktam U. Burkhanov[*,†,¶], **Dildora J. Khaydarova**[†,‖], **Rano A. Mannapova**[‡,**] **and Meerimai Zh. Karbekova**[§,††]

[†]*Tashkent State University of Economics, Tashkent, Uzbekistan*

[‡]*Tashkent Financial Institute, Tashkent, Uzbekistan*

[§]*International University named after K.Sh. Toktomamatov, Jalal-Abad, Kyrgyzstan*

[¶]*a.burkhanov@tsue.uz*

[‖]*hajdarovadildora3@gmail.com*

[**]*mannapova2019@list.ru*

[††]*meerimai.karbekova@mail.ru*

Abstract: This research aims to determine the possibilities of reducing technological barriers in the global markets for ICT goods to ensure digital inclusiveness in international entrepreneurship. To achieve the research goal, the authors conduct a factor analysis of digital

[*]Corresponding author.

inclusiveness in the global markets for ICT goods using correlation and regression analysis. As a result, based on the experience of the top 20 countries, which were key participants in the global market for ICT goods in 2023, the authors developed an econometric model of digital inclusiveness in entrepreneurship through the prism of technological barriers in the global markets for ICT goods. The constructed model holds theoretical significance as it made it possible to select globalization directions that positively and consistently impact digital inclusiveness. The model is valuable for forecasting. It allows predicting how digital inclusiveness in global ICT markets will change under the influence of globalization factors. The research contributes to developing the theory of free international trade (free trade) by rethinking the essence of digital inclusiveness in entrepreneurship through the lens of market technological barriers and refining its key factors using the global markets for ICT goods as an example. The main conclusion from the conducted research is that globalization in all directions is certainly important for ensuring inclusiveness in the global ICT goods markets. However, it only partially reduces their technological barriers and makes a limited contribution to ensuring freedom of international trade in these markets. The practical significance lies in the perspective revealed in this research of increasing the inclusiveness of the global markets for ICT goods through globalization management.

Keywords: Digital inclusiveness; global markets; ICT goods; international entrepreneurship; technological barriers to markets; managing globalization.

1. Introduction

The inclusiveness of the business environment is synonymous with market freedom and is crucial for maintaining "healthy" competition and division of labor, especially in global markets. Dynamically evolving due to the Fourth Industrial Revolution, the global markets for high-tech products, particularly ICT goods markets, deserve special attention. In these markets, inclusiveness takes on a distinctive digital form, with technological barriers playing a pivotal role in its formation.

For contemporary economic systems, the digital inclusiveness of global markets for ICT goods generates a complex of significant advantages. These benefits include the opportunity for the specialization of international production in ICT goods. This makes it possible to enhance domestic entrepreneurship efficiency, strengthen digital competitiveness, diversify markets for the produced ICT goods, and capitalize economies of scale. In this scenario, a country can also establish and maintain a global reputation as a leader in the Fourth Industrial Revolution [18].

Another advantage is associated with accelerating the pace of economic growth. For countries lacking resource capabilities for participation in other markets but possessing absolute or relative competitive advantages in the production and sale of ICT goods, establishing and developing the production capability for these goods enables them to achieve a positive balance in foreign trade. This also makes it possible to more completely realize the growth and development potential of the socioeconomic systems of such countries [11].

The considered advantages include the creation of technological elevators for developing digital economies worldwide. This advantage holds the greatest interest for developing countries seeking to gain global technological leadership. Another advantage lies in developing international transport and logistics chains and routes. Even without being producers or major suppliers of ICT goods, many countries can participate in global markets for these goods by providing their territory for advantageous and convenient transit and serving as global hubs for the storage and distribution of these goods [3,14].

Finally, discussing the benefits, it is worth noting the powerful anti-crisis effect of the digital inclusiveness of global ICT goods markets. For instance, a sharp decrease in the level of digital inclusiveness of global markets for ICT goods can cause a deficit of these goods in importing countries. In the event of a change in the digital inclusiveness of markets for complementary goods, such as raw materials, materials, components, technologies, venture investments, and digital professionals involved in producing ICT goods, the production of these goods in exporting countries may be paralyzed. In this case, the deficit of ICT goods acquires a global scale and is accompanied by a proportional increase in prices [5].

The problem lies in the fact that although the benefits of the digital inclusiveness of global markets for ICT goods are evident and widely recognized, there is uncertainty regarding the factors contributing to this inclusiveness. This determines the relevance of researching the factors of digital inclusiveness in global markets and developing measures to manage these factors to enhance the level of inclusiveness. This research seeks to contribute to solving the stated problem and aims to identify opportunities for reducing technological barriers in global markets for ICT goods to ensure digital inclusiveness in international entrepreneurship.

2. Literature Review

The fundamental basis of this research is the theory of international trade freedom (free trade) [2,17]. This theory distinguishes the following three key factors of barriers in global markets that determine the freedom of international trade:

- **Economic globalization**: The integration of domestic enterprises into global supply and sales chains, the level of development of international entrepreneurship based in the country, the global competitiveness of domestic enterprises, their export potential, and the economy's dependence on imports [7,9].
- **Social globalization**: The staffing of international trade and the readiness of consumers to purchase and consume imported products [1,6].
- **Political globalization**: The existence of international trade agreements, participation in customs unions of countries, and government support for international trade [4,10].

Exports and imports of these goods attest to the digital inclusiveness of global markets for ICT goods with regard to entrepreneurship. Scholars studying global markets for ICT goods [12–13] agree that the technological barriers of contemporary global markets for ICT goods are sufficiently high and continue to rise under the influence of scientific and technological progress in the era of the Fourth Industrial Revolution.

However, the possibilities of reducing technological barriers in global markets for ICT goods are only indirectly addressed in the existing literature, remaining unclear. Particularly, it is unknown how the listed directions of globalization of socioeconomic systems specifically influence digital inclusiveness in international entrepreneurship.

This literature gap prompts the following research question: "What are the consequences of economic, social, and political globalization for the digital inclusiveness of global markets for ICT goods?" To find an answer to this research question, the authors conduct econometric modeling of digital inclusiveness in entrepreneurship through the lens of technological barriers in global markets for ICT goods.

3. Materials and Methods

This research is conducted based on a specifically formed sample of countries. It includes the top 20 countries that are key participants in the global ICT goods market in 2023. The sample is formed based on the criterion of the highest values of import (ICTim) [16] and export (ICTex) of ICT goods [15]. It comprises ten developing and ten developed countries. Additionally, the research examines globalization statistics — economic (Gec), social (Gsc), and political (Gpl) in the sample countries based on KOF statistics [8]. The statistical data for this research are summarized in Table 1.

Using the statistical data from Table 1, the authors conduct a factor analysis of the digital inclusiveness of global markets for ICT goods. The authors apply correlation analysis to assess the relationship (separately in developed and developing countries). Using regression analysis, the authors determine the dependency (across the entire sample) between the import and export of ICT goods and the combination of globalization factors.

The directions of globalization that have a positive and consistent impact on digital inclusiveness are selected (i.e., those for which positive regression coefficients are obtained with indicators of import and export of ICT goods). Multiple linear regression equations are used to determine the prospect of increasing the inclusiveness of global markets for ICT goods through globalization management. For this purpose, the regression equations are substituted with the maximum possible (100 points) values of indicators for the selected globalization directions, and the rate of increase in the values of ICT goods import and export indicators is determined.

4. Results

To determine the specifics of globalization's influence in various directions on the digital inclusiveness of global markets for ICT goods in

Table 1. Statistics on digital inclusiveness and globalization in the top 20 countries that are key contributors to the global market for ICT goods in 2023.

Category					
Country	**ICT goods imports (% total goods imports)**	**ICT goods exports (% of total goods exports)**	**Economic globalization (overall index), scores 1–100**	**Social globalization (overall index), scores 1–100**	**Political globalization (overall index), scores 1–100**
Developing countries					
Philippines	21.75	48.48	55	60	81
Singapore	32.88	34.71	94	86	68
Malaysia	27.04	32.19	74	82	85
China	23.71	25.50	45	58	90
Thailand	14.30	16.12	68	68	82
Mexico	15.19	14.36	61	71	88
Mongolia	4.53	0.01	63	61	68
UAE	12.24	8.45	87	80	65
India	9.39	2.23	42	54	92
Russia	9.99	0.52	49	68	92
Developed countries					
Korea, Rep.	16.35	29.18	64	80	91
Czech Republic	16.89	15.51	81	84	89
Netherlands	12.80	9.98	89	87	95
Iceland	7.71	0.32	70	84	59
United States	14.00	9.07	66	85	92
United Kingdom	7.56	3.68	80	88	97
Australia	10.00	0.87	65	87	87
Japan	13.08	8.61	67	79	80
Malta	9.23	16.16	86	83	72
Sweden	9.81	5.93	83	87	96

Source: Compiled by the authors based on the materials from KOF [8] and World Bank [15–16].

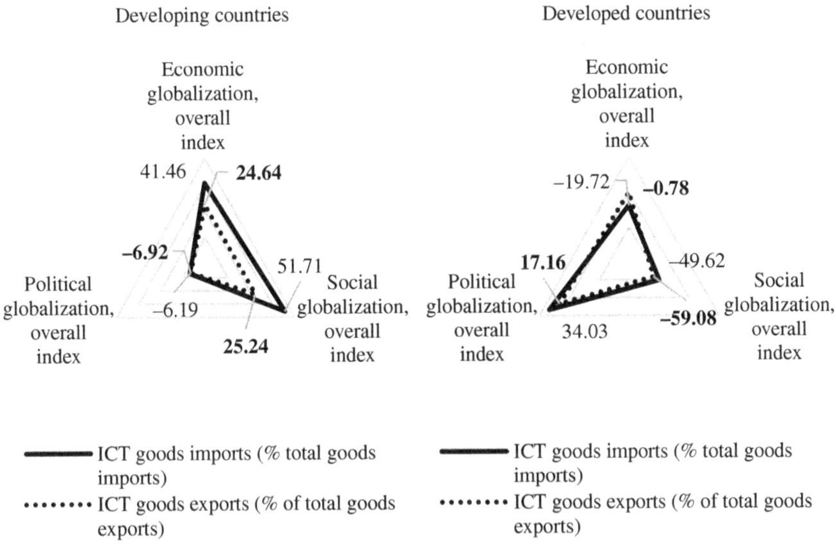

Fig. 1. Results of correlation analysis, %.

developing and developed countries, the authors conducted a correlation analysis of the data from Table 1 separately for each category of countries (Fig. 1).

The results obtained in Fig. 1 indicate that in developing countries, the import of ICT goods is most closely associated with social globalization (correlation: 51.71%) and moderately correlated with economic globalization (41.46%). Similarly, the export of ICT goods is moderately associated with social globalization (25.24%) and economic globalization (24.64%). However, political globalization negatively affects the import (–6.19%) and export (–6.92%) of ICT goods in developing countries.

In developed countries, the import of ICT goods is positively correlated only with political globalization (34.03%), as is the export of these goods (17.16%). Economic globalization negatively influences the import (–19.72%) and export (–0.78%) of ICT goods in developed countries. Similarly, social globalization negatively impacts the import (–49.62%) and export (–59.08%) of ICT goods in developed countries.

To establish more precise dependencies of import and export of ICT goods on a combination of globalization factors, the authors conducted a factor analysis of digital inclusiveness in global markets for ICT goods.

Using the regression analysis method, the following econometric model of this dependency is constructed:

$$\begin{cases} \text{ICTim} = 13.73 + 0.18 * \text{Gec} - 0.20 * \text{Gsc} + 0.04 * \text{Gpl}, \\ \text{ICTex} = 24.13 + 0.43 * \text{Gec} - 0.63 * \text{Gsc} + 0.09 * \text{Gpl}. \end{cases} \tag{1}$$

The system of equations (1) indicates that with a one-point increase in the level of economic globalization, the import of ICT goods increases by 0.18% of total commodity imports and the export of ICT goods increases by 0.43% of total commodity exports. With a one-point increase in the level of social globalization, the import of ICT goods decreases by 0.20% of total commodity imports and the export of ICT goods decreases by 0.63% of total commodity exports.

When the level of political globalization increases by one point, the import of ICT goods increases by 0.04% of total commodity imports and the export of ICT goods increases by 0.09% of total commodity exports. These results indicate the negative impact of social globalization on digital inclusiveness. The directions of globalization that have a positive and consistent impact on digital inclusiveness (i.e., those with positive regression coefficients for import and export indicators of ICT goods) are economic and political globalization.

Based on the obtained system of multiple linear regression equations, the prospect of increasing inclusiveness in global markets for ICT goods through globalization management is determined. For this purpose, Model (1) is substituted with the maximum possible (100 points) values of indicators for the selected directions of globalization, and the rate of increase in import and export values of ICT goods is determined.

As a result, it is established that with a 44.07% increase in the level of economic globalization and a 19.63% increase in the level of political globalization, there will be a growth in the volume of ICT goods imports by 42.59% (from 14.42% of total commodity imports in 2023 to 20.56% of total commodity imports). There will also be an increase in the export of ICT goods by 105.07% (from 14.09% of total commodity exports in 2023 to 28.90% of total commodity exports). Thus, the digital inclusiveness of global markets for ICT goods will increase on average by 73.83% ((42.59 + 105.07)/2).

5. Discussion

This research continues the scholarly discourse initiated by Appiah *et al.* [2] and Yu *et al.* [17], contributing to the advancement of the theory of international trade freedom (free trade) by rethinking the essence of digital inclusiveness in entrepreneurship through the lens of technological barriers in markets and refining its key factors using the example of global markets for ICT goods.

In contrast to Evstratov and Berezhnova [7] and Kusakina *et al.* [9], this research established that economic globalization, while being a crucial direction of globalization necessary for reducing barriers in global markets and ensuring freedom in international trade in ICT goods markets, is only moderately correlated with the import (41.46% correlation) and export (24.64%) of ICT goods. This correlation is observed only in developing countries. In developed countries, its influence on the digital inclusiveness of the considered markets is negative.

In contrast to Amoa-Gyarteng *et al.* [1] and Chattopadhyay and Bose [6], the authors argue that social globalization, though of decisive importance for the entry and long-term presence of developing countries in global markets for ICT goods (correlation with import: 51.71%; with export: 25.54%), serves as a constraining factor for digital inclusiveness when considering ICT goods markets as a whole, accounting for the participation of developed countries.

In contrast to Behrman [4] and Ostrovskaya *et al.* [10], the authors identified that political globalization, although a significant direction of globalization essential for reducing barriers in global markets and ensuring freedom in international trade in ICT goods markets, is only moderately correlated with the import (34.03% correlation) and export (17.16%) of ICT goods. This correlation is evident only in developed countries. In developing countries, its impact on the digital inclusiveness of the considered markets is negative.

6. Conclusion

The main conclusion from the conducted research is that globalization in all directions is undoubtedly important to ensure inclusiveness for ICT goods in the global markets. However, it only partially reduces their technological barriers and makes a limited contribution to fostering freedom in international trade in these markets.

The theoretical significance lies in the econometric model of digital inclusiveness in entrepreneurship through the lens of technological barriers in global markets for ICT goods based on the experience of the top 20 countries, which were key participants in the global market for ICT goods in 2023. The model is valuable for forecasting. It allows predicting how digital inclusiveness in global ICT markets will change under the influence of globalization factors.

The practical significance lies in the perspective revealed in this research of increasing inclusiveness in the global markets for ICT goods through globalization management. This perspective has revealed significant potential for enhancing the digital inclusiveness of these markets: global ICT product imports could increase by 42.59% and exports by 105.07%, solely due to the growth of economic and political globalization.

However, the results obtained demonstrated the limited opportunities for managing the digital inclusiveness of global markets for ICT goods through globalization regulation. This limitation is a constraint of this research. To overcome the noted limitation in future research, it is advisable to consider the influence of other factors (besides globalization) on the digital inclusiveness of global ICT goods markets, such as venture investment factors or factors related to the preparation and engagement of digital personnel in high-tech production.

References

[1] Amoa-Gyarteng, K. and Dhliwayo, S. Globalization, entrepreneurial development and unemployment: A mediation analysis in the context of South Africa. *Journal of Small Business and Enterprise Development*. 2023 December 29 [cited 2024 January 15]. DOI: 10.1108/JSBED-03-2023-0126.

[2] Appiah, M.K., Toseafa, E., Sam, A., Danso, F. and Nsowah, A. Implications of sustainability initiatives on African Continental Free Trade adoption by firms under environmental uncertainty. *International Journal of Development Issues*. 22(2): 255–277; 2023 May 17 [cited 2024 January 15]. DOI: 10.1108/IJDI-01-2023-0001.

[3] Audonin, A., Turginbayeva, A., Askerov, A. and Yergobek, D. Modern economic and logistical trends in Eurasia: How do new trans-Eurasian mega-projects influent to national economic growth. *E3S Web of Conferences*. 159: 06009; 2020 March 24 [cited 2024 January 15]. DOI: 10.1051/e3sconf/202015906009.

[4] Behrman, J.N. Obstacles to globalization: A research agenda. In: Boddewyn, J.J. (ed.), *International Business Scholarship: AIB Fellows on the First 50 Years and Beyond*. Leeds, UK: Emerald Group Publishing Limited, pp. 203–228; 2008 June 20 [cited 2024 January 15]. DOI: 10.1016/S1064-4857(08)00005-3.

[5] Bogoviz, A.V. and Ragulina, Y.V. Industry competitiveness in the new economy. In: Bogoviz, A.V. and Ragulina, Y.V. (eds.), *Industry Competitiveness: Digitalization, Management, and Integration.* Cham, Switzerland: Springer, pp. v–vi; 2020 February 24.

[6] Chattopadhyay, S. and Bose, S. Globalization and sustainable economic development: Evaluating country performances through composite rankings. In: Chandra Das, R. (ed.), *Globalization, Income Distribution and Sustainable Development.* Leeds, UK: Emerald Publishing Limited, pp. 31–46; 2022 May 25 [cited 2024 January 15]. DOI: 10.1108/978-1-80117-870-920221006.

[7] Evstratov, A.V. and Berezhnova, A.I. Development of the market of electronic payment systems in the context of accession of the Russian federation to the WTO. *World Applied Sciences Journal.* 23(1): 88–93; 2013 [cited 2024 January 15]. Available from: https://www.idosi.org/wasj/wasj23(1)13/15.pdf.

[8] KOF. Globalisation Index: Ranking 2023. 2023 [cited 2024 January 15]. Available from: https://kof.ethz.ch/en/forecasts-and-indicators/indicators/kof-globalisation-index.html.

[9] Kusakina, O.N., Bannikova, N.V., Morkovina, S.S. and Litvinova, T.N. State stimulation of development of small entrepreneurship in developing countries. *European Research Studies Journal.* 19(2SI): 276–284; 2016. Available from: https://ersj.eu/dmdocuments/16_2_p28.pdf.

[10] Ostrovskaya, V.N., Tyurina, Y.G., Konina, O.V., Przhedetskaya, N.V., Pupynina, E.G. and Natsubidze, A.S. Perspectives of elimination of "institutional gaps" in foreign economic activities of subjects of SME within the global crisis management. In: Popkova, E. (ed.), *Overcoming Uncertainty of Institutional Environment as a Tool of Global Crisis Management.* Cham, Switzerland: Springer, pp. 213–218; 2017 September 4 [cited 2024 January 15]. DOI: 10.1007/978-3-319-60696-5_26.

[11] Popkova, E.G., Bogoviz, A.V., Lobova, S.V. and Romanova, T.F. The essence of the processes of economic growth of socio-economic systems. In: Endovitsky, D. and Popkova, E. (eds.), *Management of Changes in Socio-Economic Systems.* Cham, Switzerland: Springer, pp. 123–130; 2017 December 23 [cited 2024 January 15]. DOI: 10.1007/978-3-319-72613-7_10.

[12] Singh, P. and Siddiqui, A.A. Innovation, ICT penetration, trade and economic growth in developing and developed countries: A VECM approach. *Competitiveness Review.* 33(2): 395–418; 2021 September 10 [cited 2024 January 15]. DOI: 10.1108/CR-05-2021-0074.

[13] Soylu, Ö.B., Adeleye, B.N., Ergül, M., Okur, F. and Lorente, D.B. Investigating the impact of ICT-trade nexus on competitiveness in Eastern and Western European countries. *Journal of Economic Studies.*

50(4): 773–789; 2022 June 22 [cited 2024 January 15]. DOI: 10.1108/JES-12-2021-0638.

[14] Sultanova, S.M. and Babakhanova, N.U. Statistical model for determining the quality of cargo work JSC "Uzbekistan Railways." *E3S Web of Conferences*. 402: 06016; 2023 July 19 [cited 2024 January 15]. DOI: 10.1051/e3sconf/202340206016.

[15] World Bank. ICT goods exports (% of total goods exports). [date unknown; cited 2024 January 15]. Available from: https://data.worldbank.org/indicator/TX.VAL.ICTG.ZS.UN?view=chart.

[16] World Bank. ICT goods imports (% total goods imports). [date unknown; cited 2024 January 15]. Available from: https://data.worldbank.org/indicator/TM.VAL.ICTG.ZS.UN?view=chart.

[17] Yu, G., Yang, J. and Chin, T. Free trade areas as cross-cultural knowledge-sharing platforms: Evidence from the Sino-Vietnam case. *Journal of Knowledge Management*. 26(10): 2772–2783; 2022 January 20 [cited 2024 January 15]. DOI: 10.1108/JKM-08-2021-0652.

[18] Zarova, E. and Tursunov, B. Methodology for assessing the financial security of enterprises in the post-pandemic period of digital economy. In: *Proceedings of the ICFNDS'22: The 6th International Conference on Future Networks & Distributed Systems*. New York, NY: Association for Computing Machinery, pp. 110–115; 2022 May 9 [cited 2024 January 15]. DOI: 10.1145/3584202.3584219.

Part 2

Social Manifestations of the Digital Divide and Government Regulation of Digital Inclusiveness

https://doi.org/10.1142/9789811270826_0006

Chapter 6

Public Infrastructure as the Basis of Digital Inclusiveness

Aktam U. Burkhanov[†,¶], Toir H. Sadullaev[†,‖], Elena S. Akopova[‡,] and Svetlana E. Karpushova[*,§,††]**

[†]*Tashkent State University of Economics, Tashkent, Uzbekistan*
[‡]*Rostov State University of Economics, Rostov-on-Don, Russia*
[§]*Sebryakovsky Branch of Volgograd State Technical University, Mikhaylovka, Russia*
[¶]*a.burkhanov@tsue.uz*
[‖]*t.sadullaev1990@gmail.com*
[**]*Akopova001@yandex.ru*
[††]*sfkse@yandex.ru*

Abstract: This research focuses on determining the significance of public infrastructure in terms of its elements for the digital inclusiveness of local markets and defines the prospects for achieving the most comprehensive digital inclusiveness in Russia through the development of public infrastructure. It examines the advanced and progressive experience of the top 20 countries with the highest digital inclusiveness of

[*]Corresponding author.

the economy as of 2023. The authors employ correlation and regression analysis to model the dependency and contribution of public infrastructure elements to digital inclusiveness, respectively. Additionally, a case study method is employed to analyze digital inclusiveness management through public infrastructure development using Russia as an example. The main conclusion is that the most important elements of public infrastructure for ensuring the digital inclusiveness of the contemporary economy are human resources, technological infrastructure, and institutional infrastructure. Meanwhile, general and ICT infrastructure are much less significant, and market infrastructure does not generate a positive effect in terms of increasing the digital inclusiveness of the economy. The research holds theoretical significance as the authors' conclusions facilitate the adaptation of the concept of state economic regulation to meet the current requirements of the digital economy in public infrastructure. This adaptation involves specifying the essential components of this infrastructure to ensure digital inclusiveness. The practical significance is associated with the fact that the noted perspective correlation of the level of development of public infrastructure elements in Russia for maximizing digital inclusiveness and the proposed recommendations can serve as a basis for developing a strategy to enhance digital inclusiveness in the country. The results of the conducted analysis of digital inclusiveness of the Russian economy through the prism of public infrastructure elements in 2023, identifying the strengths and weaknesses of public infrastructure, can be used to draw up a roadmap for increasing the digital inclusiveness of the Russian economy in the coming years.

Keywords: Digital inclusiveness; public infrastructure; digital economy; Russian economy; regulation of the economy.

1. Introduction

The concept of ensuring inclusiveness in economic affairs is grounded in the desire to create conducive opportunities for the fullest expression of the development potential of markets (maintaining a highly competitive environment that incentivizes the efficiency of entrepreneurial activities) and hastening the pace of economic growth. In the contemporary landscape of the digital economy, a need to ensure digital inclusiveness has emerged. Its justification is most comprehensively elucidated by the stakeholder theory.

From the standpoint of local enterprises, the advantage of digital inclusiveness in the economy lies in the opportunity to participate in local markets alongside small and medium-sized domestic businesses. An inclusive market environment helps shield local enterprises from price dumping and other forms of aggressive competition from local large enterprises and transnational corporations. Digital inclusiveness also bolsters the assurances of profitability for long-term investments in high-tech innovations.

From the perspective of foreign multinational enterprises, the digital inclusiveness of the economy is the linchpin of their entry into local markets. This becomes feasible thanks to low or even near-zero customs barriers and the general openness of local markets in the digital economy to new participants. The rejection by the national government of protectionist measures enables transnational corporations to successfully implement long-term venture investment projects, expanding their branch networks, and optimizing their supply and distribution chains.

From the viewpoint of consumers, the benefit lies in the wide variety of goods and services available, which are decreasing in price due to intense competition, improving in quality, and offered through flexible marketing propositions by sellers. Consequently, deviating from the model of digital inclusiveness in local markets is associated with numerous risks and drawbacks for consumers, including scarcity, price hikes, deterioration of quality, limited choice options, and decreased comfort in selecting and purchasing products. For a progressive society mainly acquiring products from digital markets and utilizing the opportunities of the digital economy (electronic payment for goods and services, online trading, and electronic government services), the decline in digital inclusiveness of local markets threatens a decline in the quality of life for the population.

From the perspective of society, assuming digital inclusiveness in the economy creates a much larger number of knowledge-based jobs, including those for digital professionals. This makes it possible to realize human potential and stimulate its development more completely. Additionally, the level of wages increases due to the greater power of sellers in the labor market. This ensures an improved standard of living and an increase in the population's purchasing power. Enterprises aiming for a long-term presence in the market – domestic, foreign, and even transnational corporations – seek to align with the interests of local communities (e.g., by supporting local culture and demonstrating concern for the environment).

From the government's standpoint, digital inclusiveness of local markets ensures an influx of additional tax revenues into the state budget due to a larger number of participants in these markets, their greater capacity, and the predominance of official entrepreneurship because shadow economic practices reduce competitiveness and are generally disadvantageous for enterprises in the conditions of the digital inclusiveness of markets. The pace of digital economic growth also accelerates. The country's technological sovereignty is strengthened, as in-demand high-tech goods and services are produced on its territory to a large extent.

The existing literature assigns state regulators a key role in ensuring the inclusiveness of local markets for entrepreneurship. This role is fulfilled through creating, developing, and modernizing public infrastructure. Simultaneously, it is noted that the significance of different elements of public infrastructure for inclusiveness varies greatly.

The problem lies in the uncertainty of which elements of public infrastructure are crucial for achieving and maintaining the digital inclusiveness of local markets. This reduces the effectiveness of state regulation of these markets and hinders the extraction of benefits from digital inclusiveness by all stakeholders. This has defined the aim of this research, which is to determine the significance of public infrastructure in terms of its elements for the digital inclusiveness of local markets and determine the prospect of achieving complete digital inclusiveness in Russia through the development of public infrastructure.

2. Literature Review

This research relies on the concept of state regulation of the economy, according to which the public infrastructure provided by the government determines the inclusiveness of markets for entrepreneurship [4,11]. The following universal elements of public infrastructure influencing the inclusiveness of the market environment have been identified as a result of systematizing the provisions of published scientific literature:

- Institutional infrastructure, including regulatory, legal, and other state regulation of the economy [6].
- ICT infrastructure [7–8].
- General infrastructure (fuel and energy, transport, and logistics) [1].

- Market infrastructure (economic openness, level of market competition, and investment attractiveness of the economy) [9].
- Personnel and technological infrastructure [3].

The conducted literature review showed that general issues of infrastructure provision for the contemporary economy are sufficiently elaborated in existing publications and are generally recognized as a source of inclusiveness of its markets. Additionally, the specificity of digital inclusiveness of markets has been studied only in some works by Galoyan *et al.* [2] and Kholmuminov *et al.* [5]. The role of elements of public infrastructure in the provision of digital inclusiveness is not sufficiently elaborated and is unknown. This raises the following research question (RQ): "What elements of public infrastructure make the greatest contribution to ensuring digital inclusiveness?" The search for an answer to the posed RQ is carried out in this research through econometric modeling of the dependence of digital inclusiveness of the contemporary market economy on public infrastructure in terms of its identified elements.

3. Materials and Methods

This research examines the advanced and progressive practices of the top 20 countries with the highest level of digital inclusiveness in the economy as of 2023. This international sample includes ten developed and ten developing countries, which allows the authors to consider all participants in the global markets. The research employs methods of correlation and regression analysis to assess the dependence and contribution of elements of public infrastructure to digital inclusiveness, respectively.

The research is based on official statistics from WIPO [10] for 2023. The indicator of digital inclusiveness (the outcome variable) is represented by "Business sophistication," denoted as DigInc. The following factor variables are used:

- "Institutions" as an indicator of institutional infrastructure, denoted as Iinst.
- "ICTs" as an indicator of ICT infrastructure, denoted as Iict.
- "General infrastructure" as an indicator of overall infrastructure, denoted as Igen.

- “Market sophistication” as an indicator of market infrastructure, denoted as Imark.
- “Knowledge and technology outputs” as an indicator of personnel and technological infrastructure, denoted as Ikntech.

Statistical data for these indicators in the sample are reflected in Table 1.

Table 1. Digital inclusiveness and public infrastructure in the top 20 most digitally inclusive economies in 2023, scores 1–100.

Economy	Business sophistication	Institutions	ICTs	General infrastructure	Market sophistication	Knowledge and technology outputs
Developed countries						
Sweden	75.81	74.33	86.68	64.82	59.89	63.45
USA	69.91	77.36	90.60	53.66	82.86	63.73
Singapore	69.43	98.40	94.54	57.24	67.38	55.26
Finland	65.79	85.44	94.68	60.51	58.66	61.65
Switzerland	65.50	87.33	83.74	50.52	64.42	65.30
Luxembourg	63.81	81.60	87.04	29.87	45.20	31.94
Netherlands	62.31	82.26	92.11	47.28	55.58	58.83
Republic of Korea	60.88	66.68	95.69	56.50	52.01	53.32
Belgium	60.83	68.27	70.86	50.27	47.90	46.75
Japan	59.88	72.26	90.26	48.31	61.87	51.13
Developing countries						
China	54.12	60.24	86.02	52.37	56.66	61.51
UAE	51.59	80.77	89.02	58.41	50.27	23.90
Malaysia	38.80	68.66	79.23	37.51	53.23	32.16
Philippines	37.89	46.27	53.60	26.88	37.73	29.93
Brazil	37.64	38.47	81.01	25.62	38.09	26.84
Colombia	37.30	46.67	71.53	19.33	33.36	23.65
Thailand	35.85	44.72	81.45	35.10	52.71	31.32
Russia	34.75	34.88	74.84	25.75	37.68	26.37
Saudi Arabia	34.42	59.20	85.17	43.86	47.54	21.95
Türkiye	33.54	36.48	80.52	38.54	45.06	31.14
Sample average	52.50	65.52	83.43	44.12	52.40	43.01
Sample maximum	75.81	98.40	95.69	64.82	82.86	65.30

Source: Compiled by the authors based on the WIPO materials [10].

In addition to this, the case study method is applied to conduct a case analysis of managing digital inclusiveness through the development of public infrastructure using Russia as an example. First, it includes monitoring digital inclusiveness and the level of development of public infrastructure in terms of its elements in Russia in 2023. The values of indicators in Russia and their relation to the sample's arithmetic means and maximum values are considered. Second, based on the regression analysis results, the prospective correlation of the development level of elements of public infrastructure in Russia is determined to maximize digital inclusiveness.

4. Results

To determine the relationship between the digital inclusiveness of the contemporary market economy and public infrastructure, the authors carried out econometric modeling of this dependence across the identified elements of public infrastructure. As a result, based on the experience of the top 20 countries with the highest digital inclusiveness in the economy in 2023, the following multiple linear regression model was obtained:

$$\begin{aligned}\text{DigInc} = 8.15 + 0.42 * \text{Iinst} + 0.03 * \text{Iict} + 0.04 * \text{Igen} - 0.18 * \text{Imark} \\ + 0.52 * \text{Ikntech}. \end{aligned} \quad (1)$$

Model (1) indicates that with the development of institutional infrastructure by one point, digital inclusiveness increases by 0.42 points. With the development of ICT infrastructure by one point, digital inclusiveness increases by 0.03 points. With the development of general infrastructure by one point, digital inclusiveness increases by 0.04 points. With the development of market infrastructure by one point, digital inclusiveness decreases by 0.18 points. With the development of personnel and technological infrastructure by one point, digital inclusiveness increases by 0.52 points.

In aggregate, the considered elements of public infrastructure determine the digital inclusiveness of the economy up to 93.71% (this value is accepted as the coefficient of multiple determinations). The model is reliable and significant at the 0.01 level, indicating its high quality and allowing its use in forecasting.

To further refine the extent to which contemporary public infrastructure meets the interests of ensuring digital inclusiveness in the economy, the authors conducted a case analysis of managing digital inclusiveness through the development of public infrastructure using Russia as an example. This analysis includes monitoring digital inclusiveness and the level of development of public infrastructure in terms of its elements in Russia in 2023, the results of which are shown in Fig. 1.

The monitoring results from Fig. 1 indicate that Russia has a very high level of ICT infrastructure development. This was evaluated at 74.84 points in 2023, accounting for 89.71% of the sample average and 78.22% of the sample maximum. The other elements of public infrastructure are moderately developed in Russia.

The level of development of institutional infrastructure is assessed at 35.45% of the sample maximum, general infrastructure at 39.73%, market infrastructure at 45.48%, and personnel and technological infrastructure at 40.39%. In 2023, digital inclusiveness in Russia was rated at 34.75 points, representing 66.18% of the sample average and 45.83% of the sample maximum.

Using the findings from regression analysis, the authors identified a prospective correlation between the development of public infrastructure in Russia and the potential to enhance digital inclusiveness. This finding

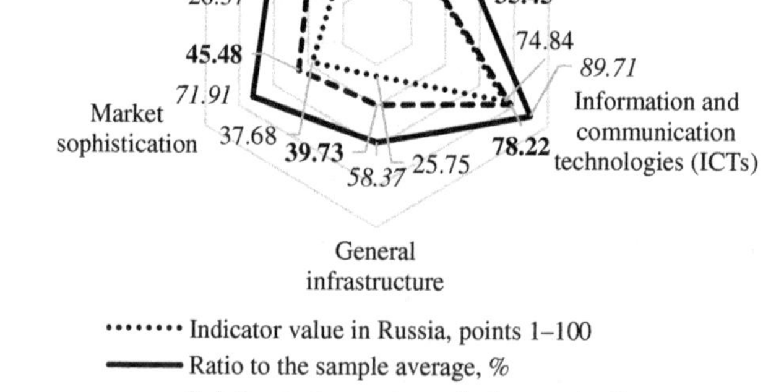

Fig. 1. Monitoring the digital inclusiveness of the Russian economy through the prism of public infrastructure elements in 2023.

allowed the authors to formulate a set of recommendations to advance public infrastructure in Russia and unlock the potential of digital inclusiveness in the Russian economy. These recommendations include the following:

- Developing institutional infrastructure by 170.08% (to 94.20 points).
- Developing ICT infrastructure by 20.04% (to 89.84 points).
- Developing general infrastructure by 15.57% (to 29.76 points).
- Developing personnel and technological infrastructure by 231.28% (to 87.37 points).

According to the authors' forecast, an increase in the digital inclusiveness of the Russian economy by 187.80% to 100 points will be achieved due to implementing the aforementioned recommendations.

5. Discussion

The contribution of the new scientific findings obtained in this research to the development of literature is evident in that they advance the concept of state regulation of the economy, clarifying the role of publicly provided infrastructure in ensuring digital inclusiveness in markets for entrepreneurship. Consequently, the research continues the scholarly discourse initiated by Gupta and Sharma [4] and Yasmeen *et al.* [11].

In contrast to Smetanina and Morozova [7] and Troshani and Rowbottom [8], the research establishes that ICT infrastructure provides a restrained effect on digital inclusiveness. Similarly, unlike Bogoviz *et al.* [1], the authors demonstrate that general infrastructure makes a weak contribution to enhancing digital inclusiveness. Unlike Wen and Zhan [9], the authors prove that market infrastructure does not exert a positive influence on digital inclusiveness.

Moreover, the results of the conducted research underscore the pivotal role and greater significance of personnel and technological infrastructure (in line with Galoyan *et al.* [3]) as well as institutional infrastructure (confirming Mbedzi *et al.* [6]) in ensuring the digital inclusiveness of the contemporary economy. Hence, it is advisable to focus efforts on these elements of public infrastructure when managing the digital inclusiveness of the economy.

6. Conclusion

The main conclusion of the conducted research is that the most important elements of public infrastructure for ensuring the digital inclusiveness of the contemporary economy are personnel and technological infrastructure, as well as the institutional infrastructure. Meanwhile, general and ICT infrastructure are much less significant, and market infrastructure does not generate a positive effect in terms of enhancing the digital inclusiveness of the economy.

The authors' conclusions possess theoretical significance as they made it possible to adapt the concept of state regulation of the economy to the contemporary needs of the digital economy in public infrastructure, specifying the key elements of this infrastructure to ensure digital inclusiveness. The obtained results also hold empirical value.

In particular, the observed perspective on the level of the development of elements of public infrastructure in Russia to maximize digital inclusiveness and the proposed recommendations may serve as a basis for developing a strategy to enhance digital inclusiveness in the country. The results of the monitoring of the digital inclusiveness of the Russian economy through the prism of elements of public infrastructure in 2023, revealing the strengths and weaknesses of public infrastructure, can be used to draft a roadmap for increasing the digital inclusiveness of the Russian economy in the coming years.

References

[1] Bogoviz, A.V., Ragulina, Y.V., Lobova, S.V. and Zhukov, B.M. Stepanova, O.M. Services infrastructure forming in the process of transport logistics stock movement. *International Review of Management and Marketing.* 6(SI6): 278–283; 2016 [cited 2024 January 15]. Available from: https://econjournals.com/index.php/irmm/article/view/2975/pdf.

[2] Galoyan, D., Mkrtchyan, T., Hrosul, V., Buhrimenko, R., Smirnova, P. and Balamut, H. Formation of adaptation strategy for business entities in the context of digital transformation of the economy. *Review of Economics and Finance.* 21(1): 616–621; 2023.

[3] Galoyan, D.R., Mayilyan, F.N., Bazinyan, Y.A., Movsisyan, M.E. and Torosyan, A.A. Triple exploitation of human capital in developing countries. In: Popkova, E.G. and Sergi, B.S. (eds.), *ESG Management of the Development of the Green Economy in Central Asia.* Cham, Switzerland:

Springer; pp. 375–383; 2023 [cited 2024 Jan 15]. DOI: 10.1007/978-3-031-46525-3_40.

[4] Gupta, S. and Sharma, A.K. Evolution of infrastructure as an asset class: A systematic literature review and thematic analysis. *Journal of Asset Management*. 23: 173–200; 2022 February 1 [cited 2024 January 15]. DOI: 10.1057/s41260-022-00255-3.

[5] Kholmuminov, S., Tursunov, B., Saidova, M., Abduhalilova, L. and Sadriddinova, N. Improving the analysis of business processes in digital era. *Proceedings of the ICFNDS 2021: The 5th International Conference on Future Networks & Distributed Systems*. New York, NY: Association for Computing Machinery, pp. 775–789; 2021 [cited 2024 January 15]. DOI: 10.1145/3508072.3508222.

[6] Mbedzi, E. and Kapingura, F.M. Infrastructure availability and disruption levels on performance of firms: A survey of Sub-Saharan Africa informal enterprises. *African Journal of Economic and Management Studies*. 14(4): 630–642; 2023 April 13 [cited 2024 January 15]. DOI: 10.1108/AJEMS-10-2022-0413.

[7] Smetanina, A.I. and Morozova, I.A. Infrastructural support of electronic payment systems markets in Russia. *Applied Econometrics and International Development*. 15(1): 57–68: 2015 January.

[8] Troshani, I. and Rowbottom, N. Corporate sustainability reporting and information infrastructure. *Accounting, Auditing & Accountability Journal*. 2023 December 13 [cited 2024 January 15]. DOI: 10.1108/AAAJ-01-2023-6244.

[9] Wen, H. and Zhan, J. New-type infrastructure and total factor productivity: Evidence from listed manufacturing firms in China. *Economic Change and Restructuring*. 56: 4465–4489; 2023 October 17 [cited 2024 January 15]. DOI: 10.1007/s10644-023-09561-1.

[10] WIPO. Global Innovation Index 2023: Innovation in the face of uncertainty. Geneva, Switzerland: WIPO; 2023 [cited 2024 January 15]. Available from: https://www.wipo.int/global_innovation_index/en/2023/.

[11] Yasmeen, R., Sarfraz, M., Shah, W.U.H., Ivascu, L. and Cifuentes-Faura, J. The impact of public awareness, infrastructure, and technological development with economic growth on solid waste management of European countries: Does governance quality matters. *Environmental Science and Pollution Research*. 30: 113442–113456, 2023 October 18 [cited 2024 January 15]. DOI: 10.1007/s11356-023-30356-4.

https://doi.org/10.1142/9789811270826_0007

Chapter 7

Regulation and Enforcement of Human Rights, Transparency, Data Protection, Ethics of Technology, and Data Use in the Context of Digital Transformation

Tatul M. Mkrtchyan[*,†,‖], **Rustam R. Rashidov**[‡,**], **Alexander A. Krutilin**[§,††] **and Rashid O. Tazhiyev**[¶,‡‡]

[†]*Armenian State University of Economics, Yerevan, Armenia*
[‡]*Alfraganus University, Tashkent, Uzbekistan*
[§]*Sebryakovsky Branch of Volgograd State Technical University, Mikhaylovka, Russia*
[¶]*Al-Farabi Kazakh National University, Almat, Kazakhstan*
[‖]*tatulmkrtchyan@yahoo.com*
[**]*rustamrr20@mail.ru*
[††]*kotyra84@bk.ru*
[‡‡]*rashidpostt@gmail.com*

Abstract: This research aims to determine the prospect of enhancing state regulation and ensuring the observance of human rights, transparency, data protection, technology ethics, and data utilization within the

[*]Corresponding author.

context of digital transformation. To achieve this, the authors conduct econometric modeling of systemic interconnections between state regulation, regulatory conditions, and the outcomes of digital economic development. The research employs regression analysis based on IMD statistics for 2023, drawing from the experiences of the top 20 countries worldwide in terms of the activity of digitalization in 2023. The principal authorial conclusion asserts that developing an e-government system is paramount in shaping a favorable regulatory environment and institutional support for the digital economy. Meanwhile, the flexibility and adaptability of state regulation play a secondary yet significant role. The scientific novelty and the originality of the research findings lie in uncovering previously unknown causal relationships between regulation, human rights compliance, transparency, data protection, technology ethics, and data utilization within the digital transformation framework. The formulated forecast and authorial recommendations possess empirical value because they pave the way for refining international practices in state regulation of the digital economy, thereby maximizing its developmental potential in the Decade of Action (until 2031).

Keywords: Government regulation; human rights enforcement; regulatory transparency; data protection; technology ethics; data use protection; digital economy.

1. Introduction

In the digital epoch of global civilization, the depth of penetration of advanced technologies into the economic practices of most entities within the world economic system is so profound that relinquishing these technologies is no longer conceivable. While automation undoubtedly entails certain costs, it has been unequivocally chosen as the vector of development for the global economy. In this high-tech context, delays in implementing digital technologies pose the risk of rendering economic systems and economic entities outsiders in international economic relations, thereby jeopardizing their competitive advantages.

In pursuing technological sovereignty, domestic production, and independence from imports, the choice of economic systems and economic entities narrows down to the preference for certain digital technologies for development and dissemination. Regardless of the chosen path in any technological segment of global markets, the efficiency and competitiveness of its participants largely hinge on their progressiveness, necessitating the accelerated creation and implementation of technologies.

The problem lies in the fact that, although the benefits and necessity of digitization are universally acknowledged and reflected in numerous published sources, issues pertaining to digitization management are only partially and separately studied. Consequently, the path of digital economic development remains unclear. Some authors [6] focus on the social factors of digitization. They note that society's readiness for change, the speed of diffusion of innovations, and the ease of learning new skills largely determine the pace of digital development of economic systems. It is also noted that the scale of production in the digital economy depends on the demand for innovative products.

Other scholars [3] highlight the significant role of economic factors in accelerating the pace of digitization and multiplying its successes. They link the digital growth of economic systems to venture investments, the development of high-tech manufacturing, and the implementation of integration mechanisms to unite the efforts of economic entities in creating and implementing digital innovations. Integration processes at the national level are also considered because they create additional opportunities for producing and selling high-tech goods and services.

Questions regarding government regulation remain much less studied. While the legal framework and institutional support are rightfully considered crucial conditions for economic development, the specific needs of the digital economy in these domains are virtually unexplored and remain unknown. Key elements of the legal framework and institutional support for developing the digital economy include ensuring the observance of human rights, transparency, data protection, technology ethics, and data usage.

However, it remains unclear to what extent the state of these elements and the possibilities for their improvement are determined by the influence of regulatory factors; the specific factors of this regulation, which are most significant for creating a favorable legal framework and institutional support for the digital economy, remain unknown. This research aims to fill the identified gap in the literature and determine the prospect of improving government regulation and ensuring the observance of human rights, transparency, data protection, technology ethics, and data usage in the context of digital transformation.

2. Literature Review

The theoretical foundation of this research is based on the concept of state regulation of the economy. In this concept, the favorability of the regulatory environment and institutional support for the digital economy are determined by the following conditions:

- Legal protection of technology application, defining the ethics of technology and the use of digital data [7].
- Protection of intellectual property rights as part of the general regulatory practice to ensure human rights compliance in the digital economy [9].
- Level of cybersecurity, determining the degree of protection of digital data [1].
- Transparency of government regulation, determining the clarity of the "rules of the game" for all participants in digital economy markets and the predictability of venture investments in digital innovations [11].

Additionally, target outcomes of government regulation of the digital economy have been identified in existing publications, including the following:

- Development of digital skills in society to expand opportunities for the dissemination and utilization of advanced technologies [10].
- Digital modernization of companies to strengthen their technological competitive advantages [2].

A literature review makes it possible to conclude that the priorities of government regulation of the digital economy are not clearly defined, and the path to achieving these priorities is not explained. Hakiman and Sheely [4] noted that due to the dynamic nature of digital economic development, government regulators need to demonstrate increased flexibility and adaptability to changing market conditions to shape a favorable regulatory environment and institutional support.

Pandey [8] suggests developing an e-government system as a special form of government regulation, which has emerged as the most effective in the context of the digital economy. However, it is unknown whether the flexibility and adaptability of government regulation or the development of the e-government system is more important for shaping a favorable regulatory environment and institutional support for the digital economy.

This is a gap in the literature, which raises the following research question (RQ): "Which factors of government regulation are most significant for ensuring compliance with human rights, transparency, data protection, technology ethics, and data usage in the context of digital transformation of the economy?"

To address the RQ, the authors conduct econometric modeling of systemic interconnections between government regulation, regulatory conditions, and the outcomes of digital economic development.

3. Materials and Methods

The authors used regression analysis to find an answer to the posed RQ, drawing upon IMD statistics [5] for 2023. With the selected method, first, the modeling of the influence of government regulation factors — "adaptability of government" (AG) as an indicator of the flexibility and adaptability of government regulation, and "e-government" (EG) as an indicator of the level of e-government system development — on the conditions of regulatory and institutional support for the digital economy is conducted:

- "Development & application of tech" (C_1) as an indicator of the legal protection of technology application.
- "Intellectual property rights" (C_2) as an indicator of intellectual property rights protection.
- "Cybersecurity" (C_3) as an indicator of the level of cybersecurity.
- "Transparency" (C_4) as an indicator of government regulation transparency.

Second, modeling is carried out to ascertain the dependence of results in the field of digital economy — "digital/technological skills" (R_1) as an indicator of the level of digital skills in society and "digital transformation in companies" (R_2) as an indicator of the activity of digital modernization of companies — on the totality of the aforementioned conditions (C_1–C_4), ensuring compliance with human rights, transparency, data protection, technology ethics, and data usage in the context of digital transformation.

For this research, the authors formed a sample from the top 20 countries in the world in terms of digitalization activity in 2023. The countries were selected based on the criterion of the highest values of AG and EG indicators. The sample includes ten developed and ten developing countries (Table 1).

Table 1. Regulation and enforcement of human rights, transparency, data protection, technology ethics, and data usage in the top 20 countries by digitalization activity in 2023.

Category	Conditions, scores 1–10				Factors		Results, scores 1–10	
Country	Development & application of technology	Intellectual property rights	Cybersecurity	Transparency	Adaptability of government policy, scores 1–10	E-government, shares from 1	Digital/Technological skills	Digital transformation in companies
Developed countries								
Denmark	8.02	8.51	7.07	7.48	6.52	0.97	8.41	7.73
Iceland	7.67	8.06	6.78	5.94	5.22	0.94	8.12	7.58
Finland	8.28	8.58	7.92	7.81	5.50	0.95	8.50	6.83
Sweden	8.00	8.25	6.38	6.92	5.42	0.94	7.90	7.49
Netherlands	7.76	8.65	7.04	6.28	5.35	0.94	8.35	6.85
USA	7.66	7.74	6.50	5.98	5.96	0.92	8.09	6.91
Belgium	7.83	7.70	7.22	6.40	6.33	0.83	7.50	7.10
Singapore	7.66	8.03	7.19	6.68	7.19	0.91	7.76	6.88
Norway	6.71	7.22	5.88	6.39	5.14	0.89	7.33	6.71
Czech Republic	6.60	7.79	6.85	7.06	5.62	0.81	7.26	6.60
Developing countries								
Qatar	7.94	7.61	8.18	7.42	7.53	0.71	8.14	7.68
Saudi Arabia	8.06	7.37	8.16	7.47	7.69	0.85	8.24	7.66
Bahrain	7.58	5.97	7.38	6.45	6.72	0.77	8.46	6.29
China	6.98	6.32	7.13	5.43	6.98	0.81	7.74	6.87
India	7.04	6.09	6.17	5.88	6.24	0.59	7.28	6.83
Jordan	7.20	6.20	6.92	5.25	5.40	0.61	7.84	6.72
Indonesia	7.13	6.14	6.14	5.61	6.48	0.72	6.89	7.02
UAE	7.34	6.22	7.07	6.36	7.97	0.90	7.48	6.30
Thailand	6.73	6.40	5.98	3.93	4.66	0.77	6.74	6.16
Malaysia	6.81	6.75	6.08	5.03	5.74	0.77	7.12	5.87

Source: Compiled by the authors based on IMD materials [5].

The modeling results are used to make the authors' forecast of the development of the digital economy in the Decade of Action (until 2030) through the improvement of state regulation of human rights, transparency, data protection, ethics of technology, and data use in the context of digital transformation. To make the forecast, the maximum possible values of AG and EG indicators are substituted into the regression equations; the consequences of this for the other indicators are determined.

4. Results

To determine the impact of government regulation factors on the favorability of regulatory and institutional conditions for developing the digital economy, the authors conducted a regression analysis of data from Table 1. As a result, the following system of equations, representing the model of government regulation ensuring compliance with human rights, transparency, data protection, technology ethics, and data usage in the context of digital transformation, was obtained:

$$\begin{cases} C_1 = 4.43 + 0.18 * AG + 2.31 * EG, & R_2 = 58.14\%; \\ C_2 = 3.23 - 0.17 * AG + 6.14 * EG, & R_2 = 76.39\%; \\ C_3 = 3.22 + 0.43 * AG + 1.21 * EG, & R_2 = 61.66\%; \\ C_4 = 0.36 + 0.42 * AG + 3.98 * EG, & R_2 = 61.12\%. \end{cases} \quad (1)$$

Model (1) showed that with a one-point increase in the flexibility and adaptability of government regulation, legal protection of technology applications increases by 0.18 points, intellectual property rights protection decreases by 0.17 points, cybersecurity level increases by 0.43 points, and government regulation transparency increases by 0.42 points.

With a one-point increase in the level of e-government development, legal protection of technology application increases by 2.31 points, intellectual property rights protection increases by 6.14 points, cybersecurity level increases by 1.21 points, and government regulation transparency increases by 3.98 points.

Together, both examined factors of government regulation determine the legal protection of technology application by 58.14%, intellectual property rights protection by 76.39%, cybersecurity level by 61.66%, and government regulation transparency by 61.12%.

Therefore, although the flexibility and adaptability of government regulation are significant factors, their impact on regulatory and institutional conditions for developing the digital economy is contradictory (the regression coefficient in the model for C_2 took a negative value). Therefore, for shaping a favorable regulatory environment and institutional support for the digital economy, the development of the e-government system is more important.

To determine the dependence of results in the field of the digital economy on the totality of the identified conditions (C_1–C_4) ensuring compliance with human rights, transparency, data protection, technology ethics, and data usage in the context of digital transformation, the following system of equations was compiled:

$$\begin{cases} R_1 = 1.65 + 0.53 * C_1 + 0.06 * C_2 + 0.23 * C_3 + 0.02 * C_4, & R_2 = 83.75\%; \\ R_2 = 2.42 + 0.51 * C_1 + 0.06 * C_2 - 0.09 * C_3 + 0.15 * C_4, & R_2 = 70.08\%. \end{cases} \quad (2)$$

Model (2) showed that with a one-point increase in the legal protection of technology application, the level of digital skills in society increases by 0.53 points and the activity of digital modernization of companies increases by 0.51 points. With a one-point increase in the degree of intellectual property rights protection, the level of digital skills in society increases by 0.06 points and the activity of digital modernization of companies increases by 0.06 points.

With an increase in the level of cybersecurity by one point, the level of digital skills in society increases by 0.23 points. However, the activity of digital modernization of companies decreases by 0.09 points. When transparency of government regulation increases by one point, the level of digital skills in society increases by 0.02 points and the activity of digital modernization of companies increases by 0.15 points.

In aggregate, the conditions ensuring compliance with human rights, transparency, data protection, technology ethics, and data usage in the context of digital transformation determine the level of development of digital skills in society by 83.75% and the activity of digital modernization of companies by 70.08%. Model (1) and model (2) served as the basis for formulating the authors' forecast for developing the digital economy in the Decade of Action (until 2030) through the improvement of government regulation (Fig. 1).

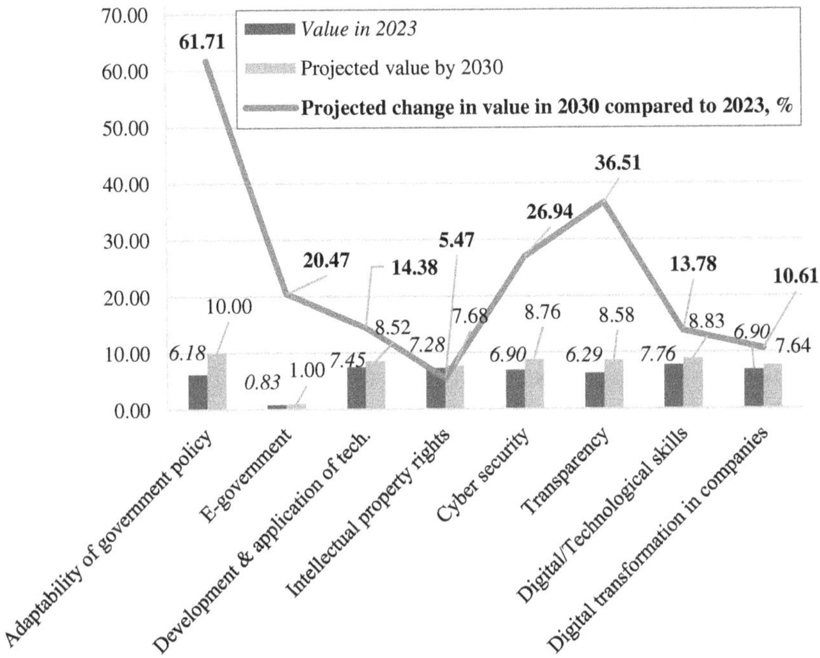

Fig. 1. Forecast of the digital economy development until 2030.

As shown in Fig. 1, optimizing the impact of government regulation factors makes the following possible:

- To increase the legal protection of technology application by 14.38% (from 7.45 points in 2023 to 8.52 points by 2030).
- To increase the level of intellectual property rights protection by 5.47% (from 7.28 points in 2023 to 7.68 points by 2030).
- To enhance cybersecurity level by 26.94% (from 6.90 points in 2023 to 8.76 points by 2030).
- To improve the transparency of government regulation by 36.51% (from 6.29 points in 2023 to 8.58 points by 2030).

Due to the enhancement of government regulation ensuring compliance with human rights, transparency, data protection, technology ethics, and data usage, an increase in the level of development of digital skills in society by 13.78% (from 7.76 points in 2023 to 8.83 points by 2030) and a rise in the activity of digital modernization of companies by 10.61%

(from 6.90 points in 2023 to 7.64 points by 2030) are projected. To implement the authors' forecast, it is recommended to increase the flexibility and adaptability of government regulation by 61.71% and enhance the development level of the e-government system by 20.47%.

5. Discussion

The obtained results contribute to the literature by advancing the concept of government regulation of the economy, elucidating the logic and regularities in shaping a favorable regulatory environment and institutional framework for the digital economy. The posed research question has been answered, concluding that the development of the e-government system is of paramount importance in forming a favorable regulatory environment and institutional framework for the digital economy, corroborating Pandey's findings [8]).

In contrast to Hakiman and Sheely [4], it was established that, despite making a generally significant contribution to shaping favorable conditions for the regulatory and institutional development of the digital economy, the flexibility and adaptability of government regulation are conflicting factors in these conditions because they do not ensure the protection of intellectual property rights.

6. Conclusion

Summarizing the research results, a final conclusion can be drawn that the development of the e-government system holds paramount importance in shaping a favorable regulatory environment and institutional framework for the digital economy. The flexibility and adaptability of government regulation play a secondary yet significant role.

The theoretical significance of the research findings lies in revealing previously unknown causal relationships between regulation and ensuring compliance with human rights, transparency, data protection, technology ethics, and data usage in the context of digital transformation. The practical significance lies in the formulated forecast and the authors' recommendations because they will make it possible to enhance international practices in government regulation of the digital economy over the Decade of Action to fully unleash its development potential.

References

[1] Alqudhaibi, A., Deshpande, S., Jagtap, S. and Salonitis, K. Towards a sustainable future: developing a cybersecurity framework for manufacturing. *Technological Sustainability*. 2(4): 372–387; 2023 July 21 [cited 2024 January 18]. DOI: 10.1108/TECHS-05-2023-0022.

[2] Bogoviz, A.V., Ragulina, Y.V., Morozova, I.A. and Litvinova, T.N. Experience of modern Russia in managing economic growth. In: Endovitsky, D. and Popkova, E. (eds.), *Management of Changes in Socio-Economic Systems*. Cham, Switzerland: Springer. pp. 147–154. 2017 December 23 [cited 2024 January 18]. DOI: 10.1007/978-3-319-72613-7_13.

[3] Bogoviz, A.V., Sozinova, A.A. and Ostrovskaya, V.V. Approaches to managing economic growth of socio-economic systems. In: Endovitsky, D. and Popkova E. (eds.), *Management of Changes in Socio-Economic Systems*. Cham, Switzerland: Springer. pp. 131–137; 2017 December 23 [cited 2024 January 18]. DOI: 10.1007/978-3-319-72613-7_11.

[4] Hakiman, K. and Sheely, R. Unlocking the potential of participatory planning: How flexible and adaptive governance interventions can work in practice. *Studies in Comparative International Development*. 2023 December 21 [cited 2024 January 18]. DOI: 10.1007/s12116-023-09415-x.

[5] IMD. World Competitiveness Online: Database. [date unknown; cited 2024 January 18]. Available from: https://worldcompetitiveness.imd.org/customsearchresults/criteriaresult.

[6] Mkrtchyan, T., Bazinyan, Y., Karapetyan, N., Sargsyan, H. and Petrosyan, N. Overreactive to international markets? Pricing mechanisms and value chains in a vegetable oil market. *Proceedings on Engineering Sciences*. 5(4): 601–608; 2023 [cited 2024 January 18]. DOI: 10.24874/PES05.04.002.

[7] Morozova, I.M, Litvinova, T.N., Przhedetskaya, N.V. and Sheveleva, V.V. The problems of financing of entrepreneurship infrastructure in developing countries and their solutions. In: Popkova, E. (ed.), *The Impact of Information on Modern Humans*. Cham, Switzerland: Springer; pp. 277–283; 2018 March 6 [cited 2024 January 18]. DOI: 10.1007/978-3-319-75383-6_35.

[8] Pandey, J.K. Evaluating public service value within collaborative e-governance: A study in the Indian context. *Digital Transformation and Society*. 2023 October 30 [cited 2024 January 18]. DOI: 10.1108/DTS-08-2023-0065.

[9] Pinarbasi, F., Sonmez, Cakir, F., Güner, Gültekin, D., Yazici, M. and Adiguzel, Z. Examination of the effects of value creation, intellectual property and organizational creativity on artificial intelligence focused enterprises. *Business Process Management Journal*. 2023 [cited 2024 January 18]. DOI: 10.1108/BPMJ-07-2023-0551.

[10] Tinmaz, H., Lee, Y.-T., Fanea-Ivanovici, M. and Baber. H. A systematic review on digital literacy. *Smart Learning Environments*. 9: 21; 2022 June 8 [cited 2024 January 18]. DOI: 10.1186/s40561-022-00204-y.

[11] Turginbayeva, A.N. and Abildaev, S.T. Quantitative assessment of regional economy competitiveness (Republic of Kazakhstan case study). *Actual Problems of Economics*. 146(8): 477–485; 2013 [cited 2024 Jan 18]. Available from: http://nbuv.gov.ua/UJRN/ape_2013_8_54.

https://doi.org/10.1142/9789811270826_0008

Chapter 8

Bridging the Digital Divide in the Era of Lockdowns

Shuxratjon M. Onorboyev[†,‖], Shahlo T. Ergasheva[†,¶,], Anna N. Liberovskaya[‡,††] and Tatiana A. Dugina[*,§,‡‡]**

[†]*Tashkent State University of Economics, Tashkent, Uzbekistan*
[‡]*Sebryakovsky Branch of Volgograd State Technical University, Mikhaylovka, Russia*
[§]*State-Funded Budget Educational Institution of Higher Education, Volzhsky Institute of Economics, Pedagogy and Law, Volzhsky, Russia*
[¶]*International School of Finance Technology and Science, Tashkent, Uzbekistan*
[‖]*shuhratjon.onorboyev@tsue.uz*
[**]*shahloer@gmail.com*
[††]*annaliber1212@mail.ru*
[‡‡]*deisi79@mail.ru*

Abstract: This research aims to determine the prospect of overcoming the digital divide in the era of lockdowns through the refinement of innovation management. It explores the experiences of the top 20 most

[*]Corresponding author.

innovative economies in the world in 2023 based on the criterion of the Global Innovation Index values as assessed by WIPO. To achieve the stated objective, the authors used econometric modeling to determine the relationship between indicators of information society development and indicators of innovation financing using regression analysis. As a result, the authors concluded that overcoming the digital divide requires the optimization of the innovation financing structure, which means increasing the volume of investments from the most promising sources — government funding for R&D and foreign investments in innovation. The novelty of this research lies in its departure from a majority of existing publications, which merely measure the digital divide, instead focusing on finding ways to diminish it, for which innovation management is proposed as an innovative applied solution. The scientific novelty of the obtained results lies in the ability to reconsider the practice of innovation financing in terms of its consequences for the digital inclusiveness of contemporary society. The fundamental significance of the authors' conclusions is rooted in the fact that they have created an opportunity to manage the development of the information society — through innovation financing. The empirical value of this research is expressed in the recommendations it offers for improving Russian innovation management practices, which will aid in overcoming the digital divide in Russia. The authors' conclusions also possess social significance as they have strengthened scientific and practical support for social adaptation in the era of lockdowns by proposing recommendations for overcoming the digital divide.

Keywords: Digital divide; lockdown era; COVID-19; digital inclusiveness; Russia; social inequality; information society; digital economy.

1. Introduction

The digital divide stands as one of the most serious barriers to achieving social inclusiveness in the realm of the digital economy. Its essence, as a distinct manifestation of social inequality inherent in the digital economy, lies in households exhibiting varying levels of activity as representatives of the information society, which develops unevenly. The list of reasons for the digital divide is quite extensive.

One of its main causes is a disparity in the infrastructure support of the digital economy, resulting in fundamental discrepancies in the accessibility, reliability, and stability of digital devices among households [3,13]. Another contributing factor is the incompleteness of the modernization process of the educational system. Consequently, graduates and learners from the most progressive educational programs possess a greater proficiency in digital skills compared to those from previous educational programs and professionals who do not pursue lifelong learning [4].

The primary reasons also include the high cost of advanced digital technologies and devices, leading income inequality to spill over into the digital divide [10]. This discrepancy in household involvement in the digital economy poses a pertinent scientific and practical problem since providers of electronic goods and services operating online are displacing their offline competitors in most markets.

As a result, the most active members of the information society continue to access the goods and services they desire; the least active members experience deprivation. They observe that goods and services remain freely accessible and consumed by others but are unable to obtain them through conventional means, being unprepared for the new (electronic) method.

The described problem was further exacerbated due to the emergence of the COVID-19 pandemic in 2020, during which lockdowns were repeatedly declared worldwide. Strict quarantine measures prevented many goods and services suppliers from continuing their offline businesses. As a result, some of them exited the markets, while the remaining, and the most significant portion, transitioned to online operation formats [9].

This trend did not wane even after the end of the pandemic. The online format proved to be most advantageous for retail suppliers of goods and services because it allows suppliers to diversify markets, leverages economies of scale, and is associated with lower costs and reduced business risks. As the digital economy advances and online business formats increasingly dominate retail markets, the digital divide intensifies [11].

Given the high risks of new epidemics and pandemics in the modern world against the backdrop of critical environmental pollution and climate change, it is fair to assert that an era of lockdowns has commenced. During this era, it is particularly important to combat the digital divide because the equitable development of the information society is a key condition for reducing overall social inequality and achieving inclusiveness in socioeconomic systems.

The novelty of this research lies in its departure from a majority of existing publications, which measure the digital divide, and the research's focus on finding ways to diminish it, proposing innovation management as a pioneering applied solution. The research aims to determine the prospect of overcoming the digital divide in the era of lockdowns through the refinement of innovation management.

2. Literature Review

The fundamental basis of this research is the concept of the information society. According to this concept, innovation is the key to developing the information society. High receptivity to innovation contributes to the rapid advancement of the information society, thus avoiding or minimizing the digital divide, whereas social resistance to innovation hampers progress in the development of the information society and deepens the digital divide. Existing publications highlight the following main manifestations of the digital divide:

- Disparities in the activity of using ICT in society [2].
- Differential intensity in accessing e-government services [8].
- Variations in the degree of household involvement in electronic civil society initiatives [1].

The published literature distinguishes the following innovation management tools based on the criteria of innovation financing subjects:

- Government funding for innovation [6].
- Private business investment in innovation [14].
- Transnational corporations' investment in innovation within a country [15].
- Foreign investments in innovation [17].

However, while the digital divide phenomenon is extensively explored in existing literature, uncertainty persists regarding the possibilities of overcoming it, particularly through innovation. This gap in the literature raises a research question about the impact of innovation financing on the digital divide.

Carayannis *et al.* [5] and Guidi [7] point out that the varying susceptibility to innovation among societies and their entities is rooted in cultural and personal characteristics. Therefore, it cannot be managed; it is considered natural and immutable. According to this viewpoint, the digital divide is accepted as a given, leaving the studied problem unresolved.

Building upon existing literature, such as Sancino *et al.* [12], which emphasizes the significant contribution of innovation to the development of the information society, this research hypothesizes that innovation contributes to reducing the digital divide. The logical justification for this hypothesis is that R&D funding promotes more active creation and implementation of innovations, accelerates their diffusion, and promotes their popularization.

This research aims to test the proposed hypothesis and seeks to determine whether the development of the information society can be managed through innovation financing. To achieve this, the research examines international experiences of changes in the digital divide under the influence of identified innovation financing factors.

3. Materials and Methods

The sample for this research included the top 20 most innovative economies in the world in 2023 based on the criterion of the Global Innovation Index values as assessed by WIPO [16]. To determine the impact of innovation management on the digital divide, the authors used regression analysis to model the dependence of indicators of information society development on innovation financing indicators. The resulting variables are as follows:

- "ICT use" as an indicator of differences in the activity of ICT use in society, denoted as ICU.
- "Government's online service" as an indicator of differentiation in the intensity of receiving e-government services, denoted as GOS.
- "E-participation" as an indicator of the spread in the degree of household involvement in electronic civil society initiatives, denoted as EPT.

The following variables serve as control variables:

- "Gross expenditure on R&D" as an indicator of government innovation financing, denoted as ge.
- "GERD performed by business" as an indicator of private business innovation financing, denoted as pb.
- "Global corporate R&D investors, top 3" as an indicator of innovation financing by transnational corporations based in the country, denoted as ci.

- "GERD financed by abroad" as an indicator of foreign investments in innovation, denoted as fa.

The values of the selected indicators in the sample countries in 2023 are reflected in Table 1.

Table 1. Digital divide and innovation finance performance of the top 20 most innovative economies in the world in 2023.

Economy name	ICT use, scores 1–10	Government's online service, shares from 1	E-participation, shares from 1	Gross expenditure on R&D (% GDP)	GERD performed by business (% GDP)	Global corporate R&D investors, top 3 (million USD)	GERD financed by abroad (% GDP)
Developed countries							
Denmark	8.85	0.98	2.81	1.75	1309.62	0.89	0.16
Finland	8.56	0.98	2.99	2.06	1796.05	0.95	0.41
Germany	8.15	0.79	3.13	2.09	12389.18	0.73	0.23
Netherlands	8.16	0.90	2.26	1.52	4422.55	0.97	0.24
Republic of Korea	8.73	0.98	4.93	3.90	8900.47	0.94	0.01
Singapore	7.60	0.96	2.22	1.41	474.85	0.98	0.10
Sweden	8.59	0.90	3.35	2.41	2853.34	0.73	0.30
Switzerland	8.89	0.77	3.19	2.16	9100.19	0.70	0.19
United Kingdom	8.85	0.89	2.93	2.07	5797.83	0.95	0.35
United States	8.47	0.93	3.46	2.68	28099.99	0.91	0.23
Developing countries							
Brazil	6.62	0.90	1.17	0.00	149.22	0.90	0.00
China	7.86	0.89	2.41	1.84	13566.21	0.86	0.01
India	4.61	0.79	0.65	0.24	1384.31	0.59	0.00
Malaysia	7.54	0.76	0.95	0.46	91.74	0.68	0.06
Russian Federation	7.74	0.74	1.10	0.62	379.59	0.60	0.02
Saudi Arabia	8.50	0.82	0.46	0.00	1078.69	0.69	0.00
Thailand	7.52	0.78	1.33	0.80	0.00	0.78	0.01
Turkey	6.85	0.86	1.13	0.80	124.37	0.78	0.02
UAE	8.14	0.90	1.50	0.79	437.88	0.78	0.00
Vietnam	6.60	0.65	0.42	0.38	210.35	0.53	0.02

Source: Compiled by the authors based on WIPO materials [16].

Based on the results of regression analysis, the authors applied the simplex method to scientifically search for combinations of values of control variables that maximize the values of the resulting variables. On this basis, the authors drew up alternative scenarios for developing an information society in Russia through innovation management.

4. Results

To determine the impact of innovation management on the digital divide using the method of regression analysis, the following three models were compiled as they reveal the dependence of information society development indicators on innovation financing indicators. The first model demonstrates how changes in ICT usage within society depend on the combination of factors related to financing innovation.

$$ICU = 6.57 + 0.64 * ge - 0.18 * pb - 0.000009 * ci + 1.74 * fa. \quad (1)$$

Model (1) indicates that only two out of the four considered factors of innovation financing contribute to reducing differences in ICT use activity. When funding for innovation by the state increases by 1% of GDP, ICT use activity increases by 0.64 points. When foreign investment in innovation increases by 1% of GDP, ICT use activity increases by 1.74 points.

The coefficient of multiple correlation (R^2) in Model (1) was 0.6992. Hence, differences in ICT use activity in society by 69.92% are explained by the influence of the aggregate factors of innovation financing. The F-test passed at the significance level of 0.05, confirming the reliability of Model (1). The second model shows how the variance in the intensity of receiving e-government services depends on the combination of factors related to financing innovation.

$$ICU = 0.72 + 0.15 * ge - 0.11 * pb - 0.000001 * ci - 0.02 * fa. \quad (2)$$

Model (2) indicates that only one out of the four considered factors of innovation financing contributes to reducing the differentiation in the intensity of receiving e-government services. When funding for innovation by the state increases by 1% of GDP, the intensity of receiving e-government services increases by 0.15 points.

The coefficient of multiple correlation (R^2) in Model (2) was 0.6808. Hence, the differentiation in the intensity of receiving e-government services by 68.08% is explained by the influence of the aggregate factors of innovation financing. The F-test passed at the significance level of 0.05, confirming the reliability of Model (2). The third model shows how the variation in households' engagement in electronic initiatives of civil society depends on the combination of factors related to financing innovation.

$$\mathrm{ICU} = 0.60 + 0.20 * \mathrm{ge} - 0.16 * \mathrm{pb} - 0{,}0000003 * \mathrm{ci} + 0.78 * \mathrm{fa}. \quad (3)$$

Model (3) indicates that only two out of the four considered factors of innovation financing contribute to reducing differences in ICT use activity. When funding for innovation by the state increases by 1% of GDP, the degree of household involvement in electronic civil society initiatives increases by 0.20 points. When foreign investment in innovation increases by 1% of GDP, the degree of household involvement in electronic civil society initiatives increases by 0.78.

The coefficient of multiple correlation (R^2) in Model (3) was 0.6477. Thus, the spread in the degree of household involvement in electronic civil society initiatives by 64.77% is explained by the influence of the aggregate factors of innovation financing. The F-test passed at the significance level of 0.10, confirming the reliability of Model (3).

To determine the prospect of reducing the digital divide, based on regression models (1)–(3), the authors conducted a scientific search for combinations of values of control variables, maximizing the values of the resulting variables using the simplex method. On this basis, two alternative scenarios for developing the information society in Russia through innovation management were developed.

The first scenario assumes the openness of Russia's digital economy and active attraction of foreign investments, the share of which increases from 0.02% of GDP in 2023 to 0.05% of GDP (+160%). Additionally, this scenario envisages an increase in the volume of state financing for innovation in Russia from 1.10% of GDP in 2023 to 2.68% of GDP (+144.40%). The alternative second scenario entails maintaining the volume of foreign investments in innovation in Russia at the level of 2023 (0.02% of GDP). To overcome the digital divide under this scenario, an increase in the volume of state financing for innovation in Russia to 2.95% of GDP (+168.66%) is required.

5. Discussion

This research contributes to the literature by advancing the concept of the information society, continuing the scholarly discussions initiated by AlJanahi and Parahoo [1], Arayankalam and Krishnan [2], and Idzi and Gomes [8], and refining the role of innovation financing in overcoming the digital divide. In contrast to Carayannis *et al.* [5] and Guidi [7], the findings demonstrated that the dissemination of digital technologies in society can be managed. Therefore, improving the practice of innovation financing is advisable; the hypothesis put forward is proven, corroborating Sancino *et al.* [12].

It was proven that government financing of innovations (confirming Turginbayeva and Domalatov [6]) and foreign investments in innovations (confirming Yue [17]) contribute to reducing the digital divide. In contrast to Turginbayeva *et al.* [14], it is substantiated that the financing of innovations by private businesses does not lead to the development of the information society. Conversely, in opposition to Veselovsky *et al.* [15], it was revealed that the financing of innovations by transnational corporations based in the country does not ensure that the digital divide will be overcome.

6. Conclusion

The main conclusion drawn from the conducted research is that overcoming the digital divide requires optimizing the structure of innovation financing by increasing investments from the most promising sources – government funding for R&D and foreign investments in innovations. The scientific novelty of the results lies in their ability to reconsider the practice of innovation financing in terms of its consequences for the digital inclusiveness of contemporary society.

The theoretical significance of the authors' conclusions is associated with the opportunities they unveil for managing the development of the information society through innovation financing. The practical significance of the research is expressed in its recommendations for improving the Russian practice of innovation management, which will help overcome the digital divide in Russia. The social significance of the authors' conclusions is grounded in their reinforcement of scientific and practical support for social adaptation in the era of lockdowns, offering recommendations for overcoming the digital divide.

References

[1] AlJanahi, A. and Parahoo, S.K. Modeling customer experience with public sector smartphone apps: A mixed methods study in the UAE. *International Review on Public and Nonprofit Marketing*. 20: 813–827; 2022 November 16 [cited 2024 January 11]. DOI: 10.1007/s12208-022-00354-2.

[2] Arayankalam, J. and Krishnan, S. ICT-based country-level determinants of social media diffusion. *Information Systems Frontiers*. 25: 1881–1902; 2022 September 15 [cited 2024 January 11]. DOI: 10.1007/s10796-022-10341-x.

[3] Arkin, P., Abushova, E., Bondarenko, V. and Przdetskaya, N. The concept of "smart cities": Prospects for the telecommunications business and the current trend in the development of modern society. In: Galinina, O., Andreev, S., Balandin, S. and Koucheryavy, Y. (eds.), *Internet of Things, Smart Spaces, and Next Generation Networks and Systems* [Internet]. Cham, Switzerland: Springer; pp. 308–317; 2020 December 22 [cited 2024 January 11]. DOI: 10.1007/978-3-030-65729-1_26.

[4] Bogoviz, A.V., Shvakov, E.E., Tretyakova, O.G., Zakharov, M.Y. and Abramov, A.N. Globalization of education in the conditions of formation of the global knowledge economy: Regularities and tendencies. In: Popkova, E. (ed.), *Growth Poles of the Global Economy: Emergence, Changes and Future Perspectives*. Cham, Switzerland: Springer; p. 993–1000; 2020 August 4 [cited 2024 January 11]. DOI: 10.1007/978-3-030-15160-7_99.

[5] Carayannis, E.G., Dezi, L., Gregori, G. and Calo, E. Smart environments and techno-centric and human-centric innovations for industry and Society 5.0: A quintuple helix innovation system view towards smart, sustainable, and inclusive solutions. *Journal of the Knowledge Economy*. 13: 926–955; 2021 February 24 [cited 2024 January 11]. DOI: 10.1007/s13132-021-00763-4.

[6] Domalatov, Ye. and Turginbayeva, A. Strategic direction to support public-private partnerships in the innovation sector of Kazakhstan: Problems and prospects. *Ad Alta – Journal of Interdisciplinary Research*. 9(1): 54–61; 2019 [cited 2024 January 11] Available from: https://www.magnanimitas.cz/ADALTA/090107/papers/A_09.pdf.

[7] Guidi, S. Innovation commons for the data economy. *Digital Society*. 2: 31; 2023 August 1 [cited 2024 January 11]. DOI: 10.1007/s44206-023-00059-x.

[8] Idzi, F.M. and Gomes, R.C. Digital governance: Government strategies that impact public services. *Global Public Policy and Governance*. 2: 427–452; 2022 November 15 [cited 2024 January 11]. DOI: 10.1007/s43508-022-00055-w.

[9] Inshakova, A.O., Sozinova., A.A. and Litvinova, T.N. Corporate fight against the COVID-19 risks based on technologies of industry 4.0 as a new

direction of social responsibility. *Risks*. 9(12): 212; 2021 November 29 [cited 2024 January 11]. DOI: 10.3390/risks9120212.

[10] Khasanov, B.A., Eshboev, U.T., Hasanova, R.B, Mukumov, Z.A., Alikulov, A.I. and Djumanova, A.B. Calculation of the invested capital profitability in the financial condition analysis process. *International Journal of Advanced Science and Technology*. 28(14): 42–48; 2019.

[11] Litvinova, T.N. Risks of Entrepreneurship amid the COVID-19 crisis. *Risks*. 10(8): 163. 2022 August 11 [cited 2024 January 11]. DOI: 10.3390/risks10080163.

[12] Sancino, A., Scognamiglio, F., Corvo, L., Inperiale, F. and Pasi, G. Institutionalizing Experimental Places for Inclusive Social Innovation: From Utopias to Heterotopias. *VOLUNTAS: International Journal of Voluntary and Nonprofit Organizations*. 2023 June 12 [cited 2024 January 11]. DOI: 10.1007/s11266-023-00584-w.

[13] Smetanina, A.I. and Morozova, I.A. Infrastructural support of electronic payment systems markets in Russia. *Applied Econometrics and International Development*. 15(1): 57–68; 2015 [cited 2024 January 11]. Available from: https://www.usc.es/economet/reviews/aeid1515.pdf.

[14] Turginbayeva, A., Ustemorov, A., Akhmetova, G., Kose, Zh., Imashev, A. and Gimranova, G. Financing aspects of an effective strategy for innovative enterprise development. *Journal of Advanced Research in Law and Economics*. 9(2): 714–720; 2018 December 12.

[15] Veselovsky, M.Y., Izmailova, M.A., Bogoviz, A.V., Lobova, S.V. and Alekseev, A.N. Business environment in Russia and its stimulating influence on innovation activity of domestic companies. *Journal of Applied Economic Sciences*. 12(7): 1967–1981; 2017.

[16] WIPO. Global Innovation Index 2023: Innovation in the face of uncertainty. Geneva, Switzerland: WIPO; 2024 [cited 2024 January 11]. Available from: https://www.wipo.int/edocs/pubdocs/en/wipo-pub-2000-2023-en-main-report-global-innovation-index-2023-16th-edition.pdf.

[17] Yue, W. Foreign direct investment and the innovation performance of local enterprises. *Humanities and Social Sciences Communications*. 9: 252; 2022 August 2 [cited 2024 January 11]. DOI: 10.1057/s41599-022-01274-6.

https://doi.org/10.1142/9789811270826_0009

Chapter 9

Digital Economy and its Inclusiveness

Diana R. Galoyan[†,‖], Aktam U. Burkhanov[‡,], Shahtibyby K. Ishembaeva[§,††] and Mukaddas Sh. Ergasheva[*,¶,‡‡]**

[†]*Armenian State University of Economics, Yerevan, Armenia*
[‡]*Tashkent State University of Economics, Tashkent, Uzbekistan*
[§]*Osh Technological University named after M.M. Adyshev, Osh, Kyrgyzstan*
[¶]*Tashkent State University of Economics, Tashkent, Uzbekistan*
[‖]*dianagaloyan@yahoo.com*
[**]*a.burkhanov@tsue.uz*
[††]*shahtibyby@mail.ru*
[‡‡]*muqaddas.ergasheva.95@bk.ru*

Abstract: This research is dedicated to solving the problem of ensuring inclusiveness in the digital economy, towards which a crucial step is the precise measurement of inclusiveness. The research aims to form a comprehensive scientific understanding of the inclusiveness of the digital economy and quantitatively measure this inclusiveness systemically. The authors explore international empirical experience and conduct a

[*]Corresponding author.

quantitative analysis of the inclusiveness of the digital economy based on official statistics for 2023. The primary method employed in this research is variance analysis. First, in the countries leading in the Fourth Industrial Revolution, the digitalization of economic sectors occurs much less evenly than in countries that joined this revolution later, where the balance of digitalization across economic sectors is highest. Second, differences in the level of digitalization of the economy among countries within established categories are significant; the categories are homogeneous, especially the category of countries leading the Fourth Industrial Revolution. Third, although generally significant, differences in the level of digitalization among countries worldwide are critical only in the category of countries leading the Fourth Industrial Revolution. As a result, the authors conclude that the problem of ensuring inclusiveness in the digital economy is most acute in the countries leading the Fourth Industrial Revolution and is weakly expressed in countries that joined later than others. The theoretical significance of the obtained results lies in the fact that they formed a systemic scientific representation of the inclusiveness of the digital economy in the uniformity of digitalization across sectors, countries, and categories of countries. The practical significance of the research findings is expressed in the fact that they essentially represent the results of comprehensive monitoring of the inclusiveness of the digital economy in 2023. The results of the conducted monitoring are useful for improving contemporary practices of developing and implementing state policies in the field of digitalization management and combating inequality.

Keywords: Digital economy; inclusiveness; inequality of countries; inequality of digitalization; fourth industrial revolution; scientific and technological progress.

1. Introduction

The digital economy is an economic–technological environment in which contemporary society operates and evolves. Initially, the very idea of transitioning to a digital economy emerged and was implemented as a means for leaders in the scientific and technological fields to accelerate their development and widen the gap from competitors. From pioneering companies, the initiative quickly spread to national governments, which declared a course toward the digital economy. Thus began the Fourth Industrial Revolution.

Currently, it is fair to assert that it has reached its zenith because most countries worldwide have already joined it, the pace of growth and development of the digital economy is unprecedentedly high, and the global community's expectations for the onset of the Fifth Industrial Revolution are rising. Thus, the Fourth Industrial Revolution is anticipated to wane in the coming years. The hallmark of the current stage of the Fourth Industrial Revolution is that its most important benchmark or evaluative criterion for the digital economy is its inclusiveness.

Undoubtedly, a key argument in favor of the inclusiveness of the digital economy is the UN's global initiative for sustainable development [12], particularly aimed at combating inequality at the level of national economic systems and countries. This grand initiative aims to make the contemporary world fairer and more comfortable for everyone, thus imbued with the idea of inclusiveness. The digital economy is no exception.

The need to achieve inclusiveness in the digital economy also arose from the fact that for the most progressive countries leading scientific and technological progress, it has become disadvantageous to be exclusive participants in the global markets of the digital economy. The internal demand in these countries for high-tech products is saturated. Thus, one is required to seek sales in foreign markets to prevent overproduction crises.

The necessity for inclusiveness in the digital economy is growing as the Fifth Industrial Revolution approaches because the countries that joined the construction of the digital economy later than others risk becoming outsiders of the impending new technological revolution. In the economies of countries in the Global South, the digitalization of economic practices occurs unevenly. In practices where scientific and technological progress is natural or receives the greatest financial support, digitalization occurs rapidly.

However, in other practices characterized by resistance to scientific and technological progress and a financing deficit, the pace of digitalization is much slower. Governments are making significant efforts to accelerate this pace and enter the Fifth Industrial Revolution with systemically digitalized economies. Thus, the problem of ensuring inclusiveness in the digital economy is relevant for all participants in today's global economic system.

However, this problem remains unresolved due to the uncertainty of how inclusive the digital economy is at present. Solving the stated problem is complicated by the multitude of manifestations of inclusiveness and the fact that existing literature typically considers only some of these manifestations and provides only qualitative assessments of inclusiveness, which are approximate and subjective.

This research aims to overcome the shortcomings of the existing literature and focuses on forming a comprehensive scientific understanding of the inclusiveness of the digital economy and the systemic quantitative measurement of this inclusiveness.

2. Literature Review

The theoretical foundation of this research is based on the concept of inclusiveness in the digital economy. According to this concept, applied to the digital economy, inclusiveness entails uniformity, evenness, and balanced digitalization of economic practices, which serve the interests of sustainable development of the digital economy [2,3,5,13–14]. The accumulated knowledge on the considered concept, as reflected in the existing literature, was systematized, which makes it possible to identify the following three manifestations of inclusiveness in the digital economy, delineated by industry and geographical criteria.

The first manifestation is the balanced digitalization of economic sectors within a country. Popkova *et al.* [6–7] suggest that the digitalization of economic sectors in countries leading the Fourth Industrial Revolution occurs more evenly than in countries that joined this revolution later. This assumption is based on the idea that leading countries have already achieved significant results in digitalization by this time, and further progress occurs naturally. In countries that joined the Fourth Industrial Revolution later due to artificial involvement through governmental measures, the results of digitalization are unevenly distributed across different sectors of the economy.

The second manifestation is the uniformity of digitalization among countries within the categories to which they belong. During international comparisons, traditionally accepted categories of countries are considered, within which countries are comparable to each other. Audonin *et al.* [1] and Kholmuminov *et al.* [4] assert that differences in the level of digitalization of the economy among countries within established categories are minimal. Therefore, the categories are homogeneous.

The third manifestation is the evenness of digitalization across different sectors of the economy within country categories (i.e., the full involvement of countries in global digital competition and the uniform development of global digital markets). Although publications such as Przhedetsky *et al.* [8], Qalandarovna Abdurakhmanova *et al.* [9], and Troyanskaya *et al.* [11] recognize the universal involvement of participants in international economic relations in the Fourth Industrial Revolution, they also note that differences in the level and pace of digitalization among countries are significant.

Based on the literature review, we can conclude that despite the existence of isolated publications, a comprehensive understanding of the inclusiveness of the digital economy has not been formed, and its degree has not been quantitatively measured and, therefore, remains unclear. To overcome the limitations of existing literature, this research examines international empirical experience and conducts a quantitative analysis of the inclusiveness of the digital economy.

3. Materials and Methods

In conducting the research, the authors utilized materials from Tortoise Media [10] on international statistics, reflecting the outcomes in the realm of digitalization concerning its sectors (according to the "Global AI index" elements) and countries for the year 2023. The primary method employed in this research is variance analysis, which is conducted to determine the variation in the following levels of digitalization:

- **Among economic sectors within a country**: The variation in the overall level of digitalization among countries within a category indicates the inclusiveness of the country's digital economy;
- **Among countries within the categories to which they belong**: The variation in the level of digitalization across different economic sectors in each country reflects the inclusiveness of the digital economy within that category of countries;
- **Among economic sectors within categories of countries**: The variation in the level of digitalization across different economic sectors within categories demonstrates the global inclusiveness of the digital economy and its global markets.

To comprehensively encompass international experience, this research is conducted across three categories of countries. These categories are delineated based on the position of countries in the Tortoise Media [10] ranking (i.e., by the level of digitalization) (Table 1).

Table 1. Statistics and variation of digitalization in 2023, place 1–62.

Category	Overall AI index	Talent	Infrastructure	Operating environment	Research	Development	Government strategy	Commercial	Variation by country, %
Country									
Top 5									
United States	1	1	1	28	1	1	8	1	181.20
China	2	20	2	3	2	2	3	2	139.54
Singapore	3	4	3	22	3	5	16	4	97.46
United Kingdom	4	5	24	40	5	8	10	5	101.78
Canada	5	6	23	8	7	11	5	7	66.40
Variation by Top 5, %	52.70	102.72	111.34	74.29	66.90	77.02	59.88	62.83	—
Middle 5									
India	14	2	59	12	30	21	38	13	76.96
Russia	30	28	19	33	39	24	7	52	46.19
UAE	28	48	4	42	34	39	24	29	43.52
Saudi Arabia	31	53	20	18	37	41	1	26	56.20
Brazil	35	21	42	44	36	36	30	39	20.49
Variation by Middle 5, %	29.05	68.24	75.17	47.95	9.72	28.24	77.86	45.97	—
Low 5									
Bahrain	58	61	39	43	58	60	61	36	20.61
Pakistan	59	33	61	61	49	57	55	58	17.32
Sri Lanka	60	56	58	60	62	62	58	54	4.79
Nigeria	61	49	62	56	52	59	54	59	8.08
Kenya	62	59	60	59	60	61	56	47	8.24
Variation by Low 5, %	2.64	21.99	17.17	13.25	9.78	3.22	4.89	18.75	—
Variation by Top 15, %	28.13	64.32	67.90	45.17	28.80	36,16	47.54	42.52	—

Source: Calculated and compiled by the authors based on Tortoise Media materials [10].

In Table 1, the greater the values taken by the variation coefficients, the greater the differences in the level of digitalization of the studied objects and, therefore, the lower the digital inclusiveness.

4. Results

To determine how inclusive the contemporary digital economy is, the authors analyzed the variation of the data from Table 1. The results are summarized in Fig. 1.

In Fig. 1, the variation of the overall level of digitalization among countries within the category is defined as follows. In the Top-5 category, the arithmetic mean of the "Overall AI index" is calculated as follows: (1 + 2 + 3 + 4 + 5)/5 = 3.00; the standard deviation takes the value of 1.58 and the coefficient of variation is 52.70% (high variation). In the Middle-5 category, the arithmetic mean of the "Overall AI index" is calculated as follows: (14 + 30 + 28 + 31 + 35)/5 = 27.60; the standard deviation takes the value of 8.02 and the coefficient of variation is 29.05% (moderate variation).

In the Low-5 category, the arithmetic mean of the "Overall AI index" is calculated as follows: (58 + 59 + 60 + 61 + 62)/5 = 60.00; the standard deviation takes the value of 1.58 and the coefficient of variation is 2.64% (very low variation). Therefore, the balanced digitalization of economic

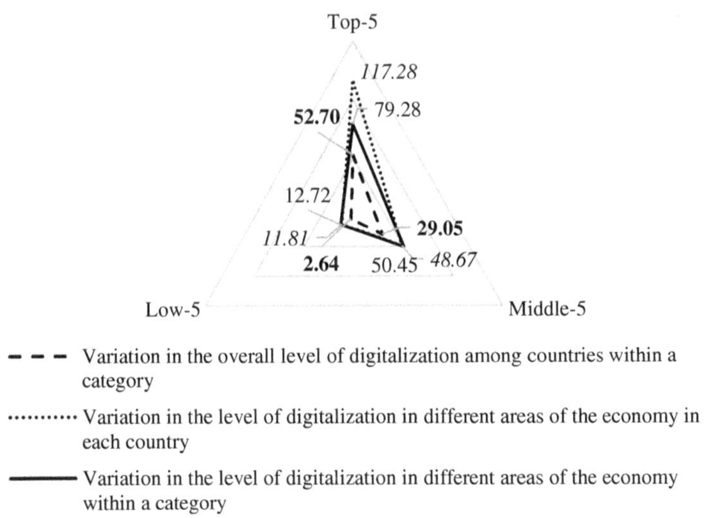

Fig. 1. Generalized results of the variation analysis (%).

sectors is highest in countries that joined the Fourth Industrial Revolution later. In countries leading this revolution, the digital economy is the least inclusive.

The variation in the level of digitalization across different economic sectors in each country is also determined as follows. The variation in the degree of digitalization of economic sectors amounted to 181.20% in the USA (very high), 139.54% in China (very high), 97.46% in Singapore (very high), 101.78% in the UK (very high), and 66.40% in Canada (high). In the Top-5 category, the arithmetic mean of the variation coefficients across economic sectors is calculated as follows: (181.20 + 139.54 + 97.46 + 101.78 + 66.40)/5 = 117.28% (very high variation).

The variation in the degree of digitalization of economic sectors amounted to 70.96% in India (high), 46.19% in Russia (moderate), 43.52% in the UAE (moderate), 56.20% in Saudi Arabia (moderate), and 20.49% in Brazil (low). In the Middle-5 category, the arithmetic mean of the variation coefficients across economic sectors is calculated as follows: (76.96 + 46.19 + 43.52 + 56.20 + 20.49)/5 = 48.68% (moderate variation).

The variation in the degree of digitalization of economic sectors amounted to 20.61% in Bahrain (low), 17.32% in Pakistan (low), 4.79% in Sri Lanka (very low), 8.08% in Nigeria (very low), and 8.24% in Kenya (very low). In the Low-5 category, the arithmetic mean of the variation coefficients across economic sectors is calculated as follows: (20.61 + 17.32 + 4.79 + 8.08 + 8.24)/5 = 11.81% (low variation).

Thus, countries that joined the Fourth Industrial Revolution later exhibit the highest level of uniformity in digitalization. Conversely, in countries at the forefront of this revolution, the digital economy is less inclusive.

The variation in the level of digitalization across different economic sectors within the category is determined as follows. In the Top-5 category, the variation in “talent” amounted to 102.72% (very high), “infrastructure” 111.34% (very high), “operating environment” 74.29% (high), “research” 66.90% (high), “development” 77.02% (high), “government strategy” 59.88% (moderate), and “commercial” 62.83% (moderate). The arithmetic mean of the variation coefficients across all digitalization areas was 79.28% (high).

In the Middle-5 category, the variation in “talent” amounted to 68.24% (moderate), “infrastructure” 75.17% (moderate), “operating environment” 47.95% (moderate), “research” 9.72% (very low), “development” 28.24% (low), “government strategy” 77.86% (high), and "commercial" 45.97% (moderate). The arithmetic mean of the variation coefficients across all digitalization areas was 50.45% (moderate).

In the Low-5 category, the variation in "talent" amounted to 21.99% (low), "infrastructure" 17.17% (low), "operating environment" 13.25% (low), "research" 9.78% (very low), "development" 3.22% (very low), "government strategy" 4.89% (very low), and "commercial" 18.75% (low). The arithmetic mean of the variation coefficients across all digitalization areas was 12.72% (very low).

Therefore, the evenness of digitalization across different economic sectors within the categories of countries is highest in countries that joined the Fourth Industrial Revolution later. In countries leading this revolution, the digital economy is the least inclusive.

5. Discussion

This research contributes to developing the concept of inclusiveness in the digital economy through the systematization of its aspects. Unlike Popkova *et al.* [6–7], the authors argued that in the countries leading the Fourth Industrial Revolution, the digitalization of economic sectors occurred much less uniformly than in countries that joined this revolution later, where the balance of digitalization across economic sectors is higher.

In contrast to Audonin *et al.* [1] and Kholmuminov *et al.* [4], the research demonstrated that the differences in the level of digitalization among countries within established categories are quite significant; the categories are homogeneous, especially in the category of leading countries of the Fourth Industrial Revolution. Unlike Przhedetsky *et al.* [8], Qalandarovna Abdurakhmanova *et al.* [9], and Troyanskaya *et al.* [11], this research established that differences in the level of digitalization among countries worldwide, although generally significant, are critical only in the category of countries leading the Fourth Industrial Revolution.

6. Conclusion

The research results show that the issue of ensuring inclusiveness in the digital economy is most acute in countries leading the Fourth Industrial Revolution and less pronounced in countries that joined this revolution later. The variation in the overall level of digitalization among countries within each category was as follows: 52.70% in the Top-5 category, 29.05% in the Middle-5 category, and 2.64% in the Low-5 category.

The variation in the level of digitalization across different sectors of the economy in each country was as follows: 117.28% in the Top-5 category, 48.67% in the Middle-5 category, and 11.81% in the Low-5 category. The variation in the level of digitalization across different sectors of the economy within each category was as follows: 79.28% in the Top-5 category, 50.45% in the Middle-5 category, and 12.72% in the Low-5 category.

The theoretical significance of these results lies in forming a comprehensive scientific understanding of the inclusiveness of the digital economy, encompassing the uniformity of digitalization across sectors, countries, and categories of countries. The practical significance of the research findings is reflected in the fact that they essentially represent the results of a comprehensive monitoring of the inclusiveness of the digital economy in 2023. The monitoring results are valuable for improving contemporary practices of developing and implementing government policies in the management of digitalization and the fight against inequality. It is also advisable to coordinate this policy at the level of country categories to maximize success in enhancing the inclusiveness of the digital economy.

References

[1] Audonin, A., Turginbayeva, A., Askerov, A. and Yergobek, D. Modern economic and logistical trends in Eurasia: How do new trans-Eurasian mega-projects influent to national economic growth. *E3S Web of Conferences*. 159: 06009; 2020 March 24 [cited 2024 January 12]. DOI: 10.1051/e3sconf/202015906009.

[2] Gill, A.S. and Germann, S. Conceptual and normative approaches to AI governance for a global digital ecosystem supportive of the UN Sustainable Development Goals (SDGs). *AI and Ethics*. 2: 293–301; 2021 May 6 [cited 2024 January 12]. DOI: 10.1007/s43681-021-00058-z.

[3] Ji, Z., Zhao, L., Song, X. and Gao, X. Digital economy impact on inclusive green growth: intermediary and spatial spillover effects in China. *Environmental Science and Pollution Research*. 30: 123657–123678; 2023 November 22 [cited 2024 January 12]. DOI: 10.1007/s11356-023-30898-7.

[4] Kholmuminov, S., Tursunov, B., Saidova, M., Abduhalilova, L. and Sadriddinova, N. Improving the analysis of business processes in digital era. *Proceedings of the ICFNDS 2021: The 5th International Conference on Future Networks & Distributed Systems*. New York, NY: Association for Computing Machinery; pp. 775–789; 2021 [cited 2024 January 12]. DOI: 10.1145/3508072.3508222.

[5] Li, Q. Comparative literature and the digital humanities: Disciplinary issues and theoretical construction. *Humanities and Social Sciences Communications*. 9: 437; 2022 December 6 [cited 2024 January 12]. DOI: 10.1057/s41599-022-01438-4.

[6] Popkova, E., Bogoviz, A.V. and Sergi, B.S. Towards digital society management and 'capitalism 4.0' in contemporary Russia. *Humanities and Social Sciences Communications*. 8(1): 77; 2021 March 17 [cited 2024 January 12]. DOI: 10.1057/s41599-021-00743-8.

[7] Popkova, E.G., Bogoviz, A.V., Pozdnyakova, U.A. and Przhedetskaya, N.V. Specifics of economic growth of developing countries. In: Endovitsky, D. and Popkova, E. (eds.), *Management of Changes in Socio-Economic Systems*. Cham, Switzerland: Springer; p. 139–146; 2017 December 23 [cited 2024 January 12]. DOI: 10.1007/978-3-319-72613-7_12.

[8] Przhedetsky, Y.V., Przhedetskaya, N.V. and Borzenko, K.V. The role of foreign economic relations in development of digital technologies in oncological service: The experience of modern Russia. In: Popkova, E.G and Ostrovskaya, V.N, (eds.), *Meta-Scientific Study of Artificial Intelligence*. Charlotte, NC: Information Age Publishing; pp. 669–675; 2021.

[9] Qalandarovna Abdurakhmanova, G., Jeong, J.Y., Rakhimjon Ugli Oqmullayev, R. and Utkir Ugli Karimov M. The impact of tourism on employment and economic growth in Uzbekistan: An ARDL bounds testing approach. *Proceedings of the ICFNDS 2021: The 5th International Conference on Future Networks & Distributed Systems*. New York, NY: Association for Computing Machinery; pp. 431–439; 2021 [cited 2024 January 12]. DOI: 10.1145/3508072.3508158.

[10] Tortoise Media. The Global AI Index [Internet]. 2023 June 28 [cited 2024 January 12]. Available from: https://www.tortoisemedia.com/intelligence/global-ai/.

[11] Troyanskaya, M.A., Ostrovskiy, V.I., Litvinova, T.N., Matkovskaya. Y.S. and Bogoviz A.V. Possibilities and perspectives for activation of sales in the agricultural machinery market within sectorial development of Russian and European economies. In: Popkova, E (ed.), *Overcoming Uncertainty of Institutional Environment as a Tool of Global Crisis Management* [Internet]. Cham, Switzerland: Springer; p. 473–480, 2017 September 4 [cited 2024 January 12]. DOI: 10.1007/978-3-319-60696-5_60.

[12] United Nations. Sustainable development: The 17 Goals [Internet]. [date unknown; cited 2024 January 12]. Available from: https://sdgs.un.org/goals.

[13] Wang, W., He, T. and Li, Z. Digital inclusive finance, economic growth and innovative development. *Kybernetes*. 52(9): 3064–3084; 2022 February 25 [cited 2024 January 12]. DOI: 10.1108/K-09-2021-0866.

[14] Xie, Z., Ma, J., Huang, S. and Zhu, J. Digital economy and inclusive green growth: The moderating effect of government environmental regulation. *Environmental Science and Pollution Research*. 30: 107938–107955; 2023 September 25 [cited 2024 January 12]. DOI: 10.1007/s11356-023-29934-3.

https://doi.org/10.1142/9789811270826_0010

Chapter 10

Digital Inclusiveness for Sustainable Development

Aziza T. Kurbanova[†,‖], **Alexey V. Tolmachev**[‡,**],
Elena V. Patsyuk[*,§,††] **and Victoria S. Ustenko**[¶,‡‡]

[†]*The Uzbekistan State Institute of Arts and Culture, Tashkent, Uzbekistan*

[‡]*Kuban State Agrarian University named after I.T. Trubilin, Krasnodar, Russia*

[§]*Sebryakovsky Branch of Volgograd State Technical University, Mikhaylovka, Russia*

[¶]*Amrita School of Social and Behavioural Sciences, Amrita Vishwa Vidyapeetham, Amritapuri, India*

[‖]*caro_8787@mail.ru*

[**]*tolmachalex@mail.ru*

[††]*elenapatsyuk@yandex.ru*

[‡‡]*victoria.ustenko@ammachilabs.org*

Abstract: This research aims to define the prospects for managing the digital inclusiveness of society and the economy in the interests of sustainable development. The research methodology relies on correlation and regression analysis for which the authors refer to official UN statistics. Based on advanced international experience, the authors developed

[*]Corresponding author.

an econometric model for the top 20 most inclusive digital economies in the world in 2023, revealing the cause-and-effect relationships of digital inclusiveness of contemporary socioeconomic systems with the implementation of 17 Sustainable Development Goals (SDGs). The model revealed that the implementation of SDGs characterizing digital inclusiveness, such as SDGs 9 and 10, is strongly and consistently linked with advancements in implementing SDGs 3, 5, and 16. Conversely, its association with achievements in implementing SDGs 7 and 11 is less pronounced and consistent. The model shows weak or negative connections with the implementation of the remaining SDGs. Using Russia as an example, the authors identified the perspective of managing the digital inclusiveness of society and the economy in the interests of sustainable development in the Decade of Action (until 2030). Comprehensive recommendations for implementing this perspective in practice have also been proposed. The main conclusion of the authors is that flexible management of inclusiveness is necessary to ensure sustainable development in the conditions of a digital economy. The theoretical significance of the results and conclusions is expressed in that they have formed a comprehensive scientific understanding of the relationship between digital inclusiveness and sustainable development. The research contributes to the literature by adapting the sustainable development concept to the context of the Fourth Industrial Revolution. For this purpose, the research specifies the relationship between digital inclusiveness and results in the field of sustainable development. The empirical value of the authors' universal conclusions lies in the fact that they will practically ensure the systemic achievement of digital inclusiveness and implementation of SDGs. Applied recommendations for Russia identified strategic guidelines for the most complete realization of the potential for ensuring inclusiveness and sustainability of the Russian digital economy.

Keywords: Digital inclusiveness; sustainable development; sustainable development goals (SDGs); inclusive society; digital economy; Russia; decade of action.

1. Introduction

The concept of sustainable development proceeds from the premise that inclusiveness is the key to stability. Drawing on international experience predating the Fourth Industrial Revolution, this concept embraces several fundamental principles. First, there is a tendency for internal social contradictions to soften as inclusiveness grows, thereby enhancing society's resilience to internal destabilizing factors and augmenting economic development potential.

Second, as social inclusiveness increases, the capacity to withstand external destabilizing factors such as foreign intervention, competition, and global crises is reinforced, fostering more resilient development. Third, there is a correlation between the enhancement of social inclusiveness and progress in achieving Sustainable Development Goals (SDGs) [13].

However, the Fourth Industrial Revolution has altered these principles, introducing amendments to contemporary sustainable development practices. The challenge lies in the fact that within the realm of the digital economy, the aforementioned foundational premises are not always adhered to, limiting the applicability of the existing sustainable development concept. Formulated based on this concept, sustainable development forecasts became significantly less accurate due to the emergence of the digital economy, rendering management measures for sustainable development considerably less effective.

The core problem stems from integrating technologies into the social, economic, and environmental interaction system, where the nature of relationships in this altered system changes. For instance, traditional mechanisms to alleviate poverty through state subsidies for households to acquire a fixed basket of consumer goods, while still capable of equalizing living standards in society, yield weak results in addressing the digital divide.

Another example is the expansion of high-tech production and consumption volumes in the digital economy era. While this development supports certain SDGs, particularly SDG 9 by fostering Industry 4.0 and digital innovations, and SDG 8 by creating jobs for digital professionals and supporting digital economic growth, it may exert a constraining influence on several other SDGs. For instance, it complicates efforts to combat climate change under SDG 13, which is traditionally pursued through reductions in industrial production volumes.

This underscores the relevance of rethinking the concept of sustainable development in light of the new context of the Fourth Industrial Revolution. This revolution has fostered the emergence of a new form of inclusiveness — digital inclusiveness. Contemporary socioeconomic systems strive to achieve it. In the Decade of Action, it is crucial to balance the outcomes and coordinate efforts to ensure digital inclusiveness and implement Sustainable Development Goals (SDGs), and achieve both systemically. This has defined the goal of this research, which is to determine the prospects for managing the digital inclusiveness of society and the economy in the interest of sustainable development.

2. Literature Review

This research is based on the sustainable development concept. The research draws upon existing literature on the topic of sustainable development [6–7, 12]. Sustainable development is interpreted as the successful implementation of all 17 SDGs and social inclusiveness [4–5]. The criterion for social inclusiveness is the achievement of SDG 10. Additionally, materials from research on digital inclusiveness are utilized [9, 15–16]. The criteria for digital inclusiveness are the results of SDGs 9 and 10.

The fundamental postulate of the concept of sustainable development is the comprehensiveness of the 17 SDGs. Based on this postulate, publications by Burkhanov *et al.* [3] and Popkova *et al.* [10] indicate that success in ensuring digital inclusiveness stimulates progress in other areas of sustainable development. That is, an increase in results in the implementation of SDG 9 and SDG 10 accelerates the achievement of other SDGs.

In turn, Alekseev *et al.* [1], Bogoviz and Sergi [2], Litvinova [8], and Sultanova and Babakhanova [11] also note that sustainable development creates a favorable socioeconomic environment for strengthening the digital inclusiveness of economic systems. That is, the pace of implementing SDG 9 and SDG 10 accelerates as other SDGs are achieved. However, the conducted literature review revealed that, despite the multitude of publications on the individual issues studied separately, the relationship between digital inclusiveness and sustainable development is underexplored.

The uncertainty of this connection serves as a gap in the literature and raises the following two research questions (RQs):

- RQ_1: What are the consequences of implementing SDG 9 and SDG 10 for other SDGs?
- RQ_2: How does implementing other SDGs affect the implementation of SDG 9 and SDG 10?

To obtain the most accurate and reliable answers to the RQs posed, this research models the interdependence of digital inclusiveness and sustainable development using a mathematical framework based on official international statistics.

3. Materials and Methods

To most accurately reflect the current state of affairs in the Fourth Industrial Revolution, this research examines the latest international experience based on the outcomes of 2023. For the purposes of this research, the authors formed a sample from the top 20 most inclusive digital economies in the world in 2023. The sample included ten developed and ten developing countries, selected based on the criterion of the highest values of the "Goal 9 Score" and "Goal 10 Score" indicators in the UN Sustainable Development Report 2023 [14]. The statistics on the implementation of 17 SDGs in the sample countries in 2023 are reflected in Table 1.

To determine the strength of the correlation between indicators, the authors apply the method of correlation analysis to determine the interdependence of SDG 9 and SDG 10 with other SDGs. Indicators with statistically significant interdependence are selected, for which the arithmetic mean of correlation coefficients exceeds 50%. Thus, those SDGs that are linked to the digital inclusiveness of contemporary society and the economy are identified.

For the selected indicators, the method of regression analysis determines (1) the dependence of the results in the implementation of SDG 9 and SDG 10 on other selected SDGs associated with them and (2) the inverse dependence of the results of the selected SDGs on the results in the implementation of SDG 9 and SDG 10. Prospects for managing the digital inclusiveness of society and the economy in the interests of sustainable development are determined by substituting the maximum possible (or greater compared to 2023) values of indicators into the regression equations (using Russia as an example).

4. Results

The results of the correlation analysis of the data from Table 1 are shown in Fig. 1.

Table 1. Results of implementing 17 SDGs in the top 20 most inclusive digital economies in the world in 2023, scores 1–100.

Category	Goal 1 Score	Goal 2 Score	Goal 3 Score	Goal 4 Score	Goal 5 Score	Goal 6 Score	Goal 7 Score	Goal 8 Score	Goal 9 Score	Goal 10 Score	Goal 11 Score	Goal 12 Score	Goal 13 Score	Goal 14 Score	Goal 15 Score	Goal 16 Score	Goal 17 Score
Country																	
Developed countries																	
Belgium	99.5	71.2	93.4	95.3	87.8	70.6	74.0	84.3	97.1	100.0	88.1	44.9	52.9	56.7	81.8	85.8	67.4
Denmark	99.2	71.0	95.4	99.3	87.0	90.7	87.7	87.6	97.0	98.2	93.0	44.6	60.8	76.3	92.8	93.8	82.1
Finland	99.6	60.9	95.4	97.2	92.1	94.3	93.0	86.8	96.0	98.5	91.2	60.1	68.8	87.9	85.1	92.5	75.6
Sweden	98.9	63.1	96.9	99.8	91.4	95.1	98.0	85.0	97.6	95.0	90.4	56.8	70.0	69.3	80.2	88.5	85.8
Norway	99.2	60.8	97.1	98.0	92.9	83.7	98.5	85.9	92.4	99.4	91.2	39.8	20.7	74.6	74.1	91.7	94.0
Iceland	99.9	53.5	96.4	98.1	94.0	59.8	99.6	77.7	87.4	100.0	86.8	37.7	51.4	62.8	54.4	93.8	77.3
Germany	99.5	72.4	93.0	97.2	81.9	88.4	77.2	87.0	95.8	88.1	90.1	55.4	64.0	74.0	79.2	89.5	84.4
Netherlands	99.3	67.7	95.7	99.3	85.1	87.2	72.0	86.3	93.4	89.8	92.9	47.7	43.3	55.3	77.9	86.7	70.8
Korea, Rep.	99.5	82.9	92.8	92.3	66.3	74.0	70.6	85.5	99.1	82.6	87.0	73.1	69.7	55.4	54.1	77.9	64.1
France	99.7	72.4	93.2	99.6	87.8	89.3	78.6	85.3	92.8	87.5	90.5	60.5	73.8	65.7	68.8	76.1	73.1
Developing countries																	
UAE	99.7	64.8	86.2	98.2	74.3	58.0	69.2	63.7	88.3	100.0	85.4	51.9	9.8	72.7	55.5	70.4	37.1
Lebanon	98.7	56.6	74.3	99.6	45.2	66.3	61.9	54.1	73.3	84.4	60.9	80.7	86.8	65.8	57.0	51.9	30.1
Russia	98.8	59.1	80.3	97.1	67.3	75.1	64.4	81.6	75.9	79.0	83.4	80.6	69.9	53.4	66.1	47.8	74.6
Algeria	97.7	57.6	77.3	70.1	41.0	58.0	65.5	67.5	53.9	97.0	62.6	89.2	88.6	64.8	67.1	65.3	81.1
Fiji	89.7	61.2	71.2	93.6	59.0	72.4	63.4	53.3	60.4	88.1	94.0	84.6	96.0	73.1	45.8	71.8	61.4
Egypt	88.0	65.3	69.4	67.9	57.7	65.1	69.9	64.9	57.9	83.9	68.5	91.2	95.1	51.5	68.3	60.1	58.8
Thailand	98.6	58.6	79.7	98.0	70.7	76.0	72.7	77.2	67.4	73.2	86.6	80.6	81.6	64.2	60.2	62.8	62.3
Maldives	100.0	44.6	86.9	96.6	38.5	73.7	64.2	72.4	47.8	92.7	80.3	74.8	89.8	63.2	51.5	66.4	68.4
Jordan	98.7	56.9	74.4	59.1	39.8	55.2	72.9	64.6	61.0	77.0	74.3	89.1	91.4	90.4	55.1	65.4	62.5
Tunisia	97.9	61.5	78.9	93.1	51.0	63.9	70.2	62.5	55.9	80.8	65.4	86.7	93.1	63.3	70.9	60.6	76.7

Source: Calculated by the authors based on Ref. [14].

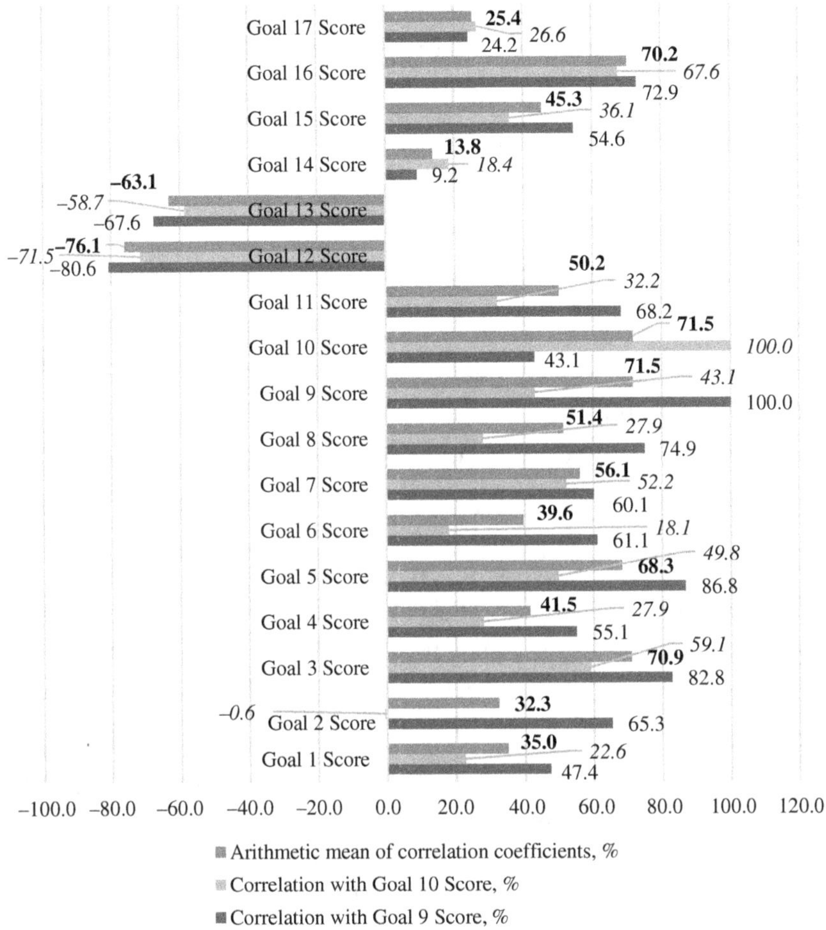

Fig. 1. Results of correlation analysis (%).

The results obtained in Fig. 1 allowed the authors to select indicators with statistically significant interdependence with digital inclusiveness as follows: The overall correlation of SDG 3 (G3S) with indicators of digital inclusiveness amounted to 70.9%; the correlation of SDG 5 (G5S) was 68.3%; the correlation of SDG 7 (G7S) was 56.1%; the correlation of SDG 11 (G14S) was 50.2%; and the correlation of SDG 16 (G16S) was 70.2%.

For the selected indicators, regression analysis found the following: (1) the dependence of the results in the implementation of SDG 9 (G9S) and SDG 10 (G10S) on the other selected SDGs associated with them;

(2) the inverse dependence of the results of the selected SDGs on the results in the implementation of G9S and G10S. The obtained results are summarized in Model (1):

$$\begin{cases} G3S = 26.98 + 0.38 * G9S + 0.32 * G10S, \\ G5S = -30.8 + 0.88 * G9S + 0.35 * G10S, \\ G7S = 9.11 + 0.32 * G9S + 0.46 * G10S, \\ G11S = 47.43 + 0.40 * G9S + 0.04 * G10S, \\ G16S = -28.26 + 0.44 * G9S + 0.76 * G10S, \\ G9S = 7.26 + 0.79 * G10S + 0.75 * G5S - 0.48 * G7S - 0.24 * G11S \\ \qquad + 0.11 * G16S, \\ G10S = 74.03 + 0.14 * G10S + 0.08 * G5S - 0.147 * G7S - 0.35 * G11S \\ \qquad + 0.51 * G16S. \end{cases} \tag{1}$$

All equations for G3S in Model (1) correspond to a significance level of 0.01, except for the last equation (for G10S), which corresponds to a significance level of 0.10. This indicates the reliability of Model (1). Based on Model (1), the authors established that both indicators of digital inclusiveness have a positive impact on the implementation of SDG 3, 5, 7, 11, and 16. Simultaneously, the influence of SDG 7 and SDG 11 on the digital inclusiveness of contemporary socioeconomic systems is negative.

Using Model (1), the authors evaluated the potential for sustainable development by increasing the level of digital inclusiveness within Russia's socioeconomic framework during the Decade of Action (up to 2030). This perspective is obtained by substituting the maximum possible values of indicators into the first five regression equations in Model (1) (i.e., with an increase in the results in the implementation of SDG 9 by 31.67% and SDG 10 by 32.14%). Thanks to this, the following benefits are achieved in Russia:

- Improvement of the healthcare system (increase in the result in the implementation of SDG 3 to 97.86 points compared to 80.26 points in 2023) by 21.94%.
- Increase in gender equality through expanding opportunities for women (increase in the result in the implementation of SDG 5 to 98.07 points compared to 67.29 points in 2023) by 45.73%.

- Strengthening energy security in combination with the development of clean energy (increase in the result in the implementation of SDG 7 to 82.55 points compared to 64.42 points in 2023) by 28.14%.
- Green economic growth of sustainable cities and regions (increase in the result in the implementation of SDG 11 to 94.71 points compared to 83.36 points in 2023) by 13.62%.
- Increase in the efficiency of institutions (increase in the result in the implementation of SDG 16 to 68.80 points compared to 47.76 points in 2023) by 44.04%.

Second, there lies the prospect of unlocking the potential for digital inclusiveness growth through the sustainable development of Russia's socioeconomic system in the Decade of Action (until 2030). This outlook is attained by substituting significantly higher values of the factor variables compared to 2023 into the last two regression equations in Model (1). The authors revealed that to achieve full (100 points) digital inclusiveness (increasing SDG 9 (+50.05% compared to 2023) and SDG 10 (+26.64%)), the optimization of sustainable development management in Russia is feasible as follows:

- Improving the healthcare system (increase in the result in the implementation of SDG 3 to 94.77 points) by 18.09%.
- Enhancing gender equality through expanding opportunities for women (increase in the result in the implementation of SDG 5 to 97.13 points) by 44.34%.
- Enhancing the efficiency of institutions (increase in the result in the implementation of SDG 16 to 71.75 points) by 50.24%.

Meanwhile, energy security and the results in the development of clean energy (SDG 7 = 64.42 points), as well as the results in the green economic development of sustainable cities and regions (SDG 11 = 83.36 points), may remain at the level of 2023.

5. Discussion

The contribution of this research to the literature lies in adapting the concept of sustainable development to the contemporary context of the Fourth Industrial Revolution. For this purpose, the research clarifies the relationship between digital inclusiveness and the results in the field of sustainable development. This research agrees with the results of Dörffel and Schuhmann [4], Fiandrino *et al.* [5], Folqué *et al.* [6], Khemani and Kumar [7], Müller [9], Turginbayeva *et al.* [12], Xia [15], and Zarrabeitia-Bilbao *et al.* [16], addressing both RQs posed.

The new scientific results obtained in this research provided an answer to RQ_1 and allowed the authors to prove that, unlike Burkhanov *et al.* [3] and Popkova *et al.* [10], success in ensuring digital inclusiveness stimulates progress only in specific areas of sustainable development. An increase in results in the implementation of SDG 9 and SDG 10 accelerates the achievement of SDG 3, 5, 7, 11, and 16 only. The consequences for the rest of the SDGs are of little significance or negative.

In contrast to Alekseev *et al.* [1], Bogoviz and Sergi [2], Litvinova [8], and Sultanova and Babakhanova [11], the research provided an answer to RQ_2 and allowed the authors to justify that progress in some areas of sustainable development creates a favorable socioeconomic environment for strengthening the digital inclusiveness of economic systems. The pace of implementing SDG 9 and SDG 10 accelerates as SDG 3, 5, and 16 are achieved, but not all SDGs. The consequences of implementing the remaining SDGs for the digital inclusiveness of modern socioeconomic systems are of little significance or negative.

6. Conclusion

The results of the conducted research can be summarized as follows:

(1) Based on the advanced international experience of the top 20 most inclusive digital economies in the world in 2023, the authors developed an econometric model, revealing the causal relationships between the digital inclusiveness of contemporary socioeconomic systems and their implementation of the 17 SDGs. The model demonstrated that the implementation of SDG 9 and SDG 10, which characterize digital inclusiveness, is most closely and consistently associated with progress in achieving SDG 3, 5, and 16, less closely and inconsistently linked with success in implementing SDG 7 and 11, and weakly or negatively associated with the implementation of the remaining SDGs;

(2) Using Russia as an example, the authors identified the perspective of managing the digital inclusiveness of society and the economy in the interest of sustainable development in the Decade of Action (until 2030). Comprehensive recommendations have also been proposed for realizing this perspective in practice.

Summarizing the results of the conducted research, the main conclusion can be drawn that ensuring sustainable development in the context of the digital economy requires flexible management of its inclusiveness. The theoretical significance of the obtained results, and the authors' conclusions based on them, is expressed in that they have formed a comprehensive scientific understanding of the relationship between digital inclusiveness and sustainable development.

The empirical value of the authors' universal conclusions lies in ensuring the systemic achievement of digital inclusiveness and the implementation of the SDGs in practice. The managerial significance of the applied recommendations for Russia is justified by the fact that they identified strategic objectives and proposed benchmark statistical values for the most complete realization of the potential for ensuring inclusiveness and sustainability in Russia's digital economy.

References

[1] Alekseev, A.N., Lobova, S.V., Bogoviz, A.V. and Ragulina, Y.V. Digitalization of the Russian energy sector: State-of-the-art and potential for future research. *International Journal of Energy Economics and Policy*. 9(5): 274–280; 2019 July 23 [cited 2024 January 14]. DOI: 10.32479/ijeep.7673.

[2] Bogoviz, A.V. and Sergi, B.S. Will the circular economy be the future of Russia's growth model? In: Sergi, B.S. (ed.), *Exploring the Future of Russia's Economy And Markets*. Leeds, UK: Emerald Publishing Limited; pp. 125–141; 2018. DOI: 10.1108/978-1-78769-397-520181007.

[3] Burkhanov, A.U., Tursunov, B., Uktamov, K. and Usmonov B. Econometric analysis of factors affecting economic stability of chemical industry enterprises in digital era: In case of Uzbekistan. *Proceeding of the ICFNDS '22: The 6th International Conference on Future Networks & Distributed Systems*. New York, NY: Association for Computing Machinery; 2023 May 9 [cited 2024 January 14]. pp. 484–490. DOI: 10.1145/3584202.3584274.

[4] Dörffel, C. and Schuhmann, S. What is inclusive development? Introducing the multidimensional inclusiveness index. *Social Indicators Research.* 162: 1117–1148; 2022 January 17 [cited 2024 January 14]. DOI: 10.1007/s11205-021-02860-y.

[5] Fiandrino, S., Scarpa, F. and Torelli, R. Fostering social impact through corporate implementation of the SDGs: Transformative mechanisms towards interconnectedness and inclusiveness. *Journal of Business Ethics.* 180: 959–973; 2022 July 12 [cited 2024 January 14]. DOI: 10.1007/s10551-022-05189-9.

[6] Folqué, M., Escrig-Olmedo, E. and Corzo Santamaría, M.T. Contribution of sustainable investment to sustainable development within the framework of the SDGS: The role of the asset management industry. *Sustainability Accounting, Management and Policy Journal.* 2022 December 21 [cited 2024 January 14]. DOI: 10.1108/SAMPJ-01-2022-0044.

[7] Khemani, P. and Kumar, D. Is financial development crucial to achieving the "2030 agenda of sustainable development"? Evidence from Asian countries. *International Journal of Emerging Markets.* 18(11): 5009–5027; 2022 February 11 [cited 2024 January 14]. DOI: 10.1108/IJOEM-06-2021-0853.

[8] Litvinova, T.N. Managing the development of infrastructural provision of AIC 4.0 on the basis of artificial intelligence: Case study in the agricultural machinery market. In: Popkova, E. and Sergi, B. (eds.), *Digital Economy: Complexity and Variety vs. Rationality.* Cham, Switzerland: Springer; pp. 317–323; 2019 September 15 [cited 2024 January 14]. DOI: 10.1007/978-3-030-29586-8_37.

[9] Müller, H. Automotive future: Digital and sustainable. *ATZ Worldwide.* 125: 4–5; 2023 July 21 [cited 2024 January 14]. DOI: 10.1007/s38311-023-1503-1.

[10] Popkova, E.G., Litvinova, T.N., Karbekova, A.B. and Petrenko, Y. Ecological behaviour in the AI economy and its impact on biodiversity: Lessons from the COVID-19 pandemic and a post-COVID perspective. *Frontiers in Environmental Science.* 10: 975861; 2022 November 29 [cited 2024 January 14]. DOI: 10.3389/fenvs.2022.975861.

[11] Sultanova, S. and Babakhanova, N. Statistical model of operational costs indicators in the intelligent transport system of JSC Uzbekistan railways. *AIP Conference Proceedings.* 2612: 060014; 2023 March 15 [cited 2024 January 14]. DOI: 10.1063/5.0119125.

[12] Turginbayeva, A.N. and Shaikh, A.A. How price sensitivity influences green consumer purchase intention? In: Vrontis, D., Weber, Y. and Tsoukatos, E. (eds.), *Proceedings of the Euromed Academy of Business: 15th Annual Conference "Sustainable Business Concepts And Practices."* Palermo, Italy: EuroMed Press; pp. 1388–1390; 2022.

[13] UN. Sustainable Development Goals. [date unknown; cited 2024 January 14]. Available from: https://www.un.org/sustainabledevelopment/.

[14] UN. Sustainable Development Report 2023. [date unknown; cited 2024 January 14]. Available from: https://dashboards.sdgindex.org/.

[15] Xia, Z. Digital interventions for a sustainable future. *Nature Reviews Psychology*. 1: 690; 2022 October 12 [cited 2024 January 14]. DOI: 10.1038/s44159-022-00125-0.

[16] Zarrabeitia-Bilbao, E., Jaca-Madariaga, M., Rio-Belver, R.-M. and Alvarez-Meaza, I. From sustainable development goals to sustainable industry, innovation and infrastructure: Insights from the digital sphere. *Environment, Development and Sustainability*. 2023 December 18 [cited 2024 January 14]. DOI: 10.1007/s10668-023-04288-5.

https://doi.org/10.1142/9789811270826_0011

Chapter 11

The Contribution of Digital Inclusiveness to the Growth of Quality of Life

Diana R. Galoyan[†,¶], **Aktam U. Burkhanov**[*,‡,‖], **Iskandar B. Jumaniyazov**[‡,**] and **Kirill Yu. Tikhomirov**[§,††]

[†]*Armenian State University of Economics, Yerevan, Armenia*
[‡]*Tashkent State University of Economics, Tashkent, Uzbekistan*
[§]*RUDN University, Moscow, Russia*
[¶]*dianagaloyan@yahoo.com*
[‖]*a.burkhanov@tsue.uz*
[**]*i.jumaniyazov@tsue.uz*
[††]*Moscowkirill@gmail.com*

Abstract: This research focuses on determining the contribution of digital inclusiveness to improving quality of life. The research methodology involves modeling the dependency of life quality components on digital inclusiveness in society using regression analysis. The research relies on UNCTAD and Numbeo statistics for the top 20 countries with the highest standard of living in the world in 2023. The authors' final

[*]Corresponding author.

conclusion is that the dissemination of advanced technologies under conditions of digital inclusiveness leads to an improvement in the quality of life but exacerbates the problem of income inequality. The theoretical significance of the results is expressed in the comprehensive examination of the consequences of the digital economy on the quality of life in all its components. It is established that while overall quality of life increases with the growth of digital inclusiveness, it also leads to an increase in the cost of living and a decrease in housing affordability for households. The research shows how digital inclusiveness influences the use of advanced technologies by households and, consequently, impacts the quality of the population's life. The practical significance of this research is justified by the perspective it reveals regarding the growth of digital inclusiveness using Russia as an example, highlighting the significant potential for improving quality of life through disseminating advanced technologies. The forecasted indicators can serve as benchmarks for conducting government monitoring of the realization of the potential for improving the quality of life through the growth of digital inclusiveness in Russia during the Decade of Science and Technology (until 2031).

Keywords: Digital inclusiveness; quality of life; technology diffusion; household well-being; smart technologies; digital economy of Russia.

1. Introduction

Scientific and technological progress has historically supported the improvement of living standards, simplifying and enhancing the comfort of economic activities, thus ensuring household prosperity. The Fourth Industrial Revolution has presented unprecedented opportunities in this regard, because in the era of the digital economy, households can delegate their routine operations to automation, freeing themselves from such work entirely for the first time. The uniqueness of the approach to automation in the digital economy lies in its individualization.

Nowadays, it is not consumers who must adapt their economic activities to contemporary automation capabilities, but smart technologies that must adapt flexibly to these changing needs. A vivid example is the intelligent curation of useful developmental information, news feeds, advertising content, and product and service offerings tailored to each consumer based on past preferences. The intellectual capabilities and applications offered by goods and service providers under conditions of open access operate in the interests of their users, which is truly revolutionary.

A prominent embodiment of advanced technologies serving households is the smart home. In it, breakthrough technological solutions aimed at enhancing quality of life are presented in various proportions but with significant concentration. A one-time initial setup is sufficient for subsequent use throughout the entire useful period of smart home technology to create coziness, comfort, and maximum convenience for its owners.

The most significant advantages of automation include one-click remote activation and remote monitoring of the state of affairs in the smart home at any convenient time for the owner. Individualization is ensured by the consumer's ability to choose the type of control for smart technologies (voice, gestures, via smartphone) and personalize the operation mode of these technologies (the ability to set the sequence of automated operations and specify the times for their execution throughout the day).

It is also important to note that these technologies are all integrated into a unified system. Acting simultaneously, smart home technologies comprehensively enhance the quality of life of their users. A promising addition to it is the smart city. Legal protection therein is guaranteed by a system of machine vision, while interactive maps help navigate the terrain and select public places to visit based on consumer interests and feedback from past visitors.

The universal accessibility to and convenience of obtaining government services are ensured by their provision in the e-government system. Services of budgetary organizations (healthcare, education) are also highly technological, progressive, and provided under conditions most favorable to consumers. However, it is unknown to what extent the benefits of scientific and technological progress are being exploited by households.

The problem lies in the fact that in the context of the digital divide, the consequences of the implementation of advanced technologies for quality of life can be neutral for society as a whole (in the case where digital technologies are disseminated in narrow circles) or even negative (in the case where households without access to advanced technologies have limited opportunities to satisfy their needs). The problem at hand points to the relevance of studying the consequences of the spread of digital technologies for quality of life. This has determined the aim of this research, which is to analyze the contribution of digital inclusiveness to improving quality of life.

2. Literature Review

This research is based on the concept of the population's quality of life, according to which the expansion of the use of advanced household technologies enhances the quality of life of the residents [1,4,12]. Content analysis of existing literature made it possible to systematize the components of quality of life and identify the potential benefits of the spread of digital technologies for enhancing the quality of life across the following identified components:

- **Purchasing power**: Smart technologies can provide intellectual support for decision-making about purchases, thereby helping to save money [10].
- **Security**: In a smart city, security is guaranteed by a system of machine vision [2].
- **Level of healthcare**: Digital healthcare improves the accessibility and quality of medical services [7].
- **Cost of living**: Automation expands opportunities for self-employment and entrepreneurship, and business automation can create high-paying jobs [9].
- **Real estate price-to-income ratio**: Smart technologies can potentially reduce the cost of housing construction, thereby lowering real estate prices [13].
- **Urban road congestion (travel time)**: Smart urban transport networks and autonomous transport allow the optimization of urban transport flows and relieve roads [8].
- **Environmental pollution**: A range of smart technologies makes it possible to reduce production and consumption waste [3].
- **Climate condition**: Many advanced technologies are climate-smart, meaning they save electricity, support decarbonization, and contribute to the fight against climate change [6].

The literature review revealed a high degree of elaboration of the issues related to quality of life in the context of the digital economy. However, existing publications pay insufficient attention to issues of digital inclusiveness in the context of studying quality of life. This gap in the literature creates ambiguity regarding the importance of digital inclusiveness for the spread of digital technology and its impact on the quality of life of the population. This prompts the following research question (RQ): "How does digital inclusiveness affect quality of life?" To find an answer to the posed RQ, this research models the dependency of the components of quality of life on digital inclusiveness in society.

3. Materials and Methods

The methodology of this research entails modeling the dependence of the components of quality of life on digital inclusiveness in society using regression analysis. The "readiness for frontier technologies index" [11] serves as the indicator of digital inclusiveness. Quantitative measurement of the level of development of the components of quality of life relies on the values of indicators within the corresponding Numbeo index [5].

The research is based on data from 2023. The sample includes the top 20 countries with the highest standard of living in the world in 2023. The sample is formed based on the criterion of the highest values of the Numbeo quality of life index [5]. To comprehensively illuminate international experience, the sample includes ten developed and ten developing countries (Table 1).

Based on the results of the regression analysis, the authors identified the prospect of improving the quality of life in Russia through the growth of digital inclusiveness in the Decade of Science and Technology (until 2031). For this purpose, the regression equations were substituted with the maximum values of the DGIN indicator, and the scale and nature of the changes in the other indicators were forecasted.

4. Results

To determine the relationship between the components of quality of life and digital inclusiveness in society using regression analysis, the authors analyzed data from Table 1. As a result, the following regression models

Table 1. Quality of life and digital inclusiveness in the top 20 countries with the highest quality of life in the world in 2023.

	Quality of life components, scores 1–100								
	Purchasing Power Index	Safety Index	Health Care Index	Cost of Living Index*	Property Price to Income Ratio*	Traffic Commute Time Index*	Pollution Index*	Climate Index	Readiness for frontier technologies index, share from 1
Category	**QL_1**	**QL_2**	**QL_3**	**QL_4**	**QL_5**	**QL_6**	**QL_7**	**QL_8**	**DGIN**
Country									
Developed countries									
Netherlands	107.80	72.70	77.10	68.60	7.20	25.50	23.70	86.80	0.94
Denmark	105.00	73.40	79.20	78.60	6.60	28.50	21.30	81.80	0.89
Switzerland	118.70	76.40	74.50	114.20	9.70	28.40	19.60	79.60	0.94
Luxembourg	127.10	64.90	75.00	73.20	11.50	29.10	21.90	82.60	0.88
Finland	98.80	73.20	77.10	67.50	7.80	27.20	12.00	59.20	0.92
Iceland	90.10	75.10	67.00	83.30	7.00	20.60	15.20	68.80	0.84
Austria	91.20	72.70	77.20	66.00	10.30	24.80	21.50	77.10	0.80
Australia	110.90	54.50	75.30	75.30	7.50	36.10	25.40	93.90	0.90
Norway	95.00	66.50	76.70	88.60	8.10	26.70	17.70	68.70	0.90
Germany	107.60	62.40	71.90	62.90	10.70	31.20	28.80	83.30	0.92
Developing countries									
Oman	108.20	80.30	58.20	47.80	3.60	22.60	37.20	67.20	0.57
UAE	123.40	84.90	69.60	60.30	3.00	36.10	48.20	45.80	0.74
Qatar	123.60	85.20	73.80	59.50	5.30	29.70	60.00	36.00	0.55
Saudi Arabia	101.90	75.40	61.20	50.60	3.00	29.40	63.30	41.40	0.65
South Africa	83.90	24.60	63.70	37.80	3.40	39.10	56.40	95.30	0.61
Uruguay	38.40	47.30	68.40	59.90	13.70	37.30	43.90	98.00	0.57
Mexico	43.50	45.60	72.50	37.30	8.40	39.30	58.50	85.80	0.58
Malaysia	65.70	47.10	70.00	35.00	8.10	37.00	61.70	57.90	0.76
Kuwait	96.70	67.40	59.70	46.80	11.50	33.40	67.80	20.20	0.64
Russia	40.90	60.70	59.70	40.80	16.30	43.90	60.90	46.00	0.76

Note: *The lower the values of these indicators, the higher the quality of life of the population.
Source: Compiled by the authors based on the materials from Numbeo [5] and UNCTAD [11].

were formulated. First, the model depicting the dependency of purchasing power on digital inclusiveness is as follows:

$$QL_1 = 39.2721 + 71.1561 * DGIN. \tag{1}$$

Model (1) indicates that with a one-point increase in the level of digital inclusiveness, purchasing power rises by 71.1561 points. The coefficient of determination has assumed a value of 37.74%, indicating a moderate correlation between the considered variables. Second, the model depicting the dependency of security on digital inclusiveness is as follows:

$$QL_2 = 47.6091 + 23.3149 * DGIN. \tag{2}$$

Model (2) reveals that with a one-point increase in the level of digital inclusiveness, security increases by 23.3149 points. The coefficient of determination has assumed a value of 21.95%, indicating a moderate correlation between the considered variables. Third, the model depicting the dependency of the healthcare level on digital inclusiveness is as follows:

$$QL_3 = 47.9290 + 29.2461 * DGIN. \tag{3}$$

Model (3) indicates that with a one-point increase in the level of digital inclusiveness, the healthcare level increases by 29.2461 points. The coefficient of determination has assumed a value of 62.49%, indicating a strong correlation between the considered variables. Fourth, the model depicting the dependency of the cost of living on digital inclusiveness is as follows:

$$QL_4 = -10.4220 + 95.2111 * DGIN. \tag{4}$$

Model (4) suggests that with a one-point increase in the level of digital inclusiveness, the cost of living increases by 95.2111 points. The coefficient of determination has assumed a value of 68.80%, indicating a strong correlation between the considered variables. Fifth, the model depicting the relationship between the housing price-to-income ratio and digital inclusiveness is as follows:

$$QL_5 = 4.4014 + 4.8615 * DGIN. \tag{5}$$

Model (5) indicates that with a one-point increase in the level of digital inclusiveness, the housing price-to-income ratio increases by 4.8615 points. The coefficient of determination has assumed a value of 19.51%, indicating a moderate correlation between the considered variables. Sixth, the model depicting the relationship between urban road congestion (travel time) and digital inclusiveness is as follows:

$$QL_6 = 42.7824 - 14.9580{*}DGIN. \tag{6}$$

Model (6) suggests that with a one-point increase in the level of digital inclusiveness, travel time decreases by 14.9580 points. The coefficient of determination has assumed a value of 34.54%, indicating a moderate correlation between the considered variables. Seventh, the model depicting the relationship between environmental pollution and digital inclusiveness is as follows:

$$QL_7 = 119.4090 - 105.6800{*}DGIN. \tag{7}$$

Model (7) indicates that with a one-point increase in the level of digital inclusiveness, environmental pollution decreases by 105.6800 points. The coefficient of determination has assumed a value of 77.91%, indicating a strong correlation between the considered variables. Eighth, the model depicting the relationship between climate conditions and digital inclusiveness is as follows:

$$QL_8 = 35.2769 + 43.6109{*}DGIN. \tag{8}$$

Model (8) suggests that with a one-point increase in the level of digital inclusiveness, the climate condition improves by 43.6109 points. The coefficient of determination has assumed a value of 28.75%, indicating a moderate correlation between the considered variables.

Based on regression models (1)–(8), the prospect of improving the quality of life in Russia through enhancing digital inclusiveness in the Decade of Science and Technology (until 2031) has been determined. For this purpose, the regression equations were fitted with the maximum values of the DGIN indicator, and the scale and nature of changes in other indicators were forecasted. The obtained results are presented in Fig. 1.

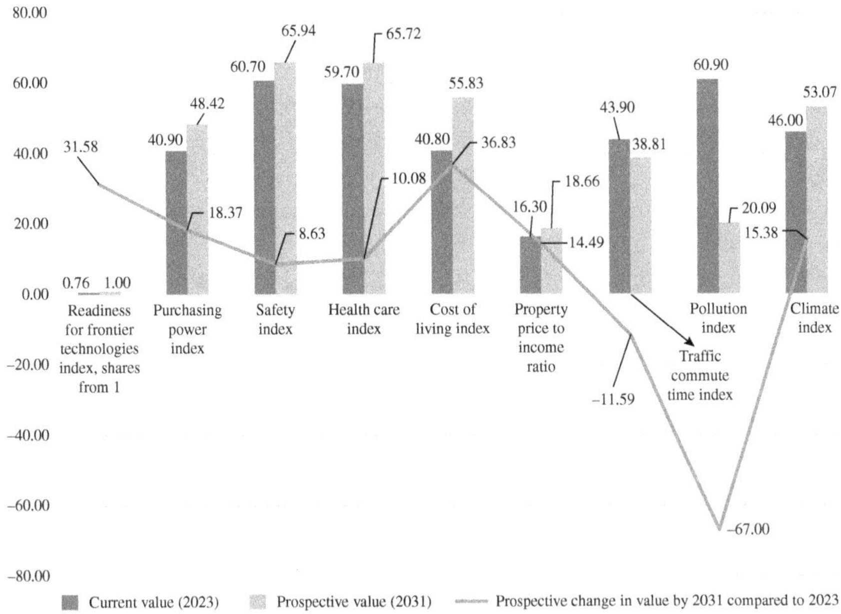

Fig. 1. Perspective of improving the quality of life in Russia through the growth of digital inclusiveness in the Decade of Science and Technology (until 2031).

The results of the authors' forecast from Fig. 1 indicate that an increase in digital inclusiveness in Russia by 31.58% will lead to the following improvements in the quality of life concerning its identified components:

- Purchasing power by 18.37%;
- Security by 8.63%;
- Healthcare level by 10.08%;
- Cost of living by 36.83%;
- Housing price-to-income ratio by 14.49%;
- Urban road congestion (travel time) by 11.59%;
- Environmental pollution by 67.00%;
- Climate condition by 15.38%.

5. Discussion

The findings of this research enhance the literature by deepening our understanding of quality of life, particularly emphasizing the importance of digital inclusiveness. This builds upon the scholarly discussion initiated by Dotsenko *et al.* [1], Lippi *et al.* [4], and Veselovsky *et al.* [12] concerning the impact of advanced technology on the quality of life of the population.

The findings provided an answer to the posed RQ, demonstrating that digital inclusiveness enhances the quality of life overall. Specifically, it increases purchasing power (confirming Tursunov [10]), enhances security (confirming Ismagilova *et al.* [2]), improves healthcare levels (confirming Przhedetskiy *et al.* [7]), reduces urban road congestion, thereby cutting travel time (confirming Sultanova and Babakhanova [8]), decreases environmental pollution (confirming Li *et al.* [3]), and ameliorates climate conditions (confirming Popkoba and Shi [6]).

However, in contrast to Torres *et al.* [9], the research found that digital inclusiveness does not decrease but rather increases the cost of living. Also, contrary to Yang *et al.* [13], the authors revealed that digital inclusiveness does not decrease but rather increases the housing price-to-income ratio. This points to the inflationary risks associated with digital inclusiveness and complicates the fight against poverty in the digital economy.

6. Conclusion

The main conclusion of this research is that the proliferation of advanced technologies in conditions of digital inclusiveness ensures an increase in the quality of life but exacerbates the problem of income inequality. The theoretical significance of the obtained results and conclusions lies in the comprehensive exploration of the impact of the digital economy on the various aspects of quality of life. Although, digital inclusiveness improves quality of life, it also increases the cost of living and reduces the affordability of housing.

The practical significance of the research is justified by the fact that the perspective of increasing digital inclusiveness presented herein, using Russia as an example, has revealed significant potential for improving the quality of life based on the dissemination of advanced technologies. The forecasted indicators can serve as benchmarks for conducting state monitoring of the realization of the potential for improving the quality of life through the growth of digital inclusiveness in Russia in the Decade of Science and Technology (until 2031).

References

[1] Dotsenko, E., Galoyan, D., Burdenko, E. and Mudrova, S. Structural inertia as a constraint for sustainable development and interregional differences in quality of life reducing. *E3S Web of Conferences*. 174: 04041; 2020 June 18 [cited 2024 January 19]. DOI: 10.1051/e3sconf/202017404041.

[2] Ismagilova, E., Hughes, L., Rana, N.P. and Dwivedi, Y.K. Security, privacy and risks within smart cities: Literature review and development of a smart city interaction framework. *Information Systems Frontiers*. 24: 393–414; 2020 July 21 [cited 2024 January 19]. DOI: 10.1007/s10796-020-10044-1.

[3] Li. W., Wang, F., Liu, T., Xue, Q. and Liu, N. Peer effects of digital innovation behavior: An external environment perspective. *Management Decision*. 61(7): 2173–2200; 2023 March 27 [cited 2024 January 19]. DOI: 10.1108/MD-06-2022-0865.

[4] Lippi, L., Turco, A., Folli, A., D`Abrosca, F., Curci, C., Mezian, K, *et al.* Technological advances and digital solutions to improve quality of life in older adults with chronic obstructive pulmonary disease: A systematic review. *Aging Clinical and Experimental Research*. 2023 Mar 23 [cited 2024 Jan 19]. DOI: 10.1007/s40520-023-02381-3.

[5] Numbeo. Quality of life index by country. 2023 [cited 2024 January 19]. Available from: https://www.numbeo.com/quality-of-life/rankings_by_country.jsp?title=2023.

[6] Popkova, E.G. and Shi, X. Economics of climate change: Global trends, country specifics and digital perspectives of climate action. *Frontiers in Environmental Economics*. 1: 935368; 2022 June 1 [cited 2024 January 19]. DOI: 10.3389/frevc.2022.935368.

[7] Przhedetskiy, Y.V., Przhedetskaya, N.V., Borzenko. K.V. and Bondarenko, V.A. Blockchain technologies in healthcare institutions: Focus on security and effective cooperation with the government. *International Journal of Economics and Business Administration*. 7: 92–99; 2019 [cited 2024 January 19]. DOI: 10.35808/ijeba/373.

[8] Sultanova, S. and Babakhanova, N. Statistical model of operational costs indicators in the intelligent transport system of JSC "Uzbekistan railways." *AIP Conference Proceedings*. 2612: 060014; 2023 March 15 [cited 2024 January 19]. DOI: 10.1063/5.0119125.

[9] Torres, A.I., Barros, C.L., da Silva, A.F. and Silva, R.J. The pay what you want pricing strategy applied to digital products: An essay. *Journal of Revenue and Pricing Management*. 21: 529–537; 2021 November 22 [cited 2024 January 19]. DOI: 10.1057/s41272-021-00355-6.

[10] Tursunov, B. Financial security in small business in period of digital economy: In case of Uzbekistan. *Proceedings of the ICFNDS '22: The 6th International Conference on Future Networks & Distributed Systems*. New York, NY: Association for Computing Machinery; pp. 491–498; 2022 [cited 2024 January 19]. DOI: 10.1145/3584202.3584275.

[11] UNCTAD. Annex A. Frontier technology trends and Annex B. Frontier technologies readiness index. In: *Technology and Innovation Report 2023*. Geneva, Switzerland: UN; 2023 [cited 2024 January 19]. Available from: https://unctad.org/system/files/official-document/tir2023ch7annex_en.pdf.

[12] Veselovsky, M.Y., Izmailova, M.A., Bogoviz, A.V., Lobova, S.V. and Alekseev, A.N. Innovative solutions for improving the quality of corporate governance in Russian companies. *Quality – Access to Success*. 19(162): 60–66; 2018.

[13] Yang, F., Ren, J. and Xia, C. Digitalisation and cream skimming adverse selection in the property-casualty insurance industry: Evidence from China. *The Geneva Papers on Risk and Insurance – Issues and Practice*. 2024 January 13 [cited 2024 January 19]. DOI: 10.1057/s41288-023-00310-z.

Part 3

Practical Solutions for Ensuring Digital Inclusiveness in Contemporary Entrepreneurial Economics

https://doi.org/10.1142/9789811270826_0012

Chapter 12

Electronic Democracy in the Information Society: Prospects for Implementation and Problems of Implementation

Igor A. Strakhov[†,§], Irina E. Belova[*,†,¶], Anna Sh. Elyazyan[†,‖], Yulya G. Yakovleva[‡,] and Anna V. Lichkovakha[†,††]**

[†]*Russian University of Cooperation,*
Mytishchi, Russia
[‡]*Financial University under the Government of the Russian Federation,*
Moscow, Russia
[§]*iast96@mail.ru*
[¶]*advbelova@mail.ru*
[‖]*elyazyan.77@mail.ru*
[**]*a.v.lichkovaha@ruc.su*
[††]*8676@apmo.ru*

Abstract: In the contemporary information society, where information technologies increasingly permeate all spheres of life, electronic democracy becomes ever more relevant and promising. This is a novel approach to citizen participation in decision-making, where the primary tools are digital platforms and Internet technologies. One of the key

[*]Corresponding author.

perspectives of implementing electronic democracy is the expansion of participation accessibility for all population segments. The Internet makes it possible to overcome geographical and social barriers, providing citizens with the opportunity to express their opinions and participate in the decision-making process irrespective of their place of residence or social status. However, despite the prospects, the implementation of electronic democracy also faces challenges, one of which is the uneven distribution of access to Internet technologies. In certain regions and for specific population groups, Internet access is limited or nonexistent, creating obstacles to participation in electronic democracy. Additionally, concerns exist regarding the security of data and the privacy of citizens. With the increased use of digital platforms, the risks of hacking attacks and leaks of confidential information grow, potentially undermining citizens' trust in electronic democracy. Another problem is the lack of awareness and the quality of the discussed issues. Electronic democracy platforms often encounter noisy and trivial discussions, complicating the decision-making process. Furthermore, there is a danger of manipulating public opinion through mass media and social networks. This research explores the key factors influencing the formation and development as well as the main problems associated with the implementation and widespread use of electronic democracy tools in Russia and across the world.

Keywords: Electronic democracy; information society; smart technologies; public participation; people power.

1. Introduction

With the advent of the Internet and social networks, people have gained new tools for expressing their opinions, exchanging information, and participating in making important state decisions.

The realities of today's society are such that technological revolutions have become an integral part of our lives, permeating all areas of activity and fundamentally changing the world. One of the fundamental changes is transforming society into an information-based one. In this context, Russia is considered one of the rapidly developing countries.

Advanced technologies, such as digitalization and informatization, penetrate every aspect of our lives. We have become dependent on smartphones, the Internet, social networks, and other means of communication. They simplify our lives and make things more accessible and comfortable.

However, in this situation, there is an increasing demand from citizens for the state to create conditions for the full implementation of democratic procedures through information systems and technologies. In these circumstances, electronic democracy becomes a relevant and integral part of the political process.

Citizens want to feel like active participants in society and have the opportunity to influence decision-making, participate in elections, and interact with the state without unnecessary obstacles. They strive for transparency and openness of government, the ability to receive up-to-date information about the activities of government bodies, and participate in them.

Electronic voting systems, public consultations, and electronic access to government services are inseparable from the information society. The government must actively develop and support such mechanisms so that citizens can fully participate in decision-making.

Society requires active participation and interaction between citizens and the government. Technological revolutions have led to an information society where everyone can express their position and participate in making important decisions. It is important for the government to understand this need and create conditions that allow citizens to fully utilize information technologies in implementing democratic procedures.

The active use of electronic systems for organizing elections and conducting surveys and discussions provides the country's population with direct access to the political process. This increases the level of civic participation and creates an open platform for discussions and collective decision-making. However, it is necessary to consider the positive aspects of the development of electronic democracy and its potential risks to data security and the protection of personal information. This research will address the main issues of the functioning of electronic democracy on a global scale, conduct a comparative analysis of electronic democracy mechanisms in some countries, and provide recommendations for their development and resolution.

2. Methodology

Russian scholars have long been examining how political institutions operate during the formation and establishment of an information society. A detailed study of these issues traces its roots to the key concepts of post-industrialism. The most renowned authors in this field are Bell, Drucker, Rismen, Kahn, Katz, Castells, McLuhan, Stonier, Tapscott, Toffler, Schrader, Webster, and others. Russian scholarship is represented by the works of Alexeev and Abramov [1], Arutyunyan [2], Avakyan [3], Belyarov [4], Botnev [5], Bronnikov [6], Gritsenko [7], Kuznetsov and Dubinets [8], Moskalenko [9], Musayev [10], Nevinsky [11], Permyakova, Platonov, and Yumaev [12], Pyrma [13], Romashkin [14], and Titov [15].

In preparing this research, the authors used general scientific methods of cognition, including dialectical, systemic–structural, formal–logical, and sociological methods, modeling, and several others (analysis, synthesis, analogy, generalization, induction, deduction, and abstraction).

The authors also applied special legal methods of understanding scientific and practical problems (formal–legal, historical–legal, comparative–legal, and statistical methods, as well as the teleological method of interpreting legal norms).

3. Results

Electronic democracy, or e-democracy, represents a new form of citizen participation in the political process through the use of information technologies. In recent decades, it has become increasingly relevant globally, generating interest from governments and society.

A historically clear example of the functioning of electronic democracy can be found in Estonia. The country pioneered the creation of a system of electronic government that allows citizens to make online statements, access information about government services, and vote in elections. As a result, digital technologies have influenced all aspects of the country's life, from the economy to social well-being.

The relevance of the emergence of electronic democracy is based on several factors. First, worldwide Internet usage has created new opportunities for communication and citizen participation in the political process. Nowadays, a majority of people have access to the Internet, making it the primary tool for exchanging information and opinions.

Second, electronic democracy offers several advantages compared to traditional forms of political participation. It allows citizens to be active participants without the need for physical presence. This is particularly important for people with limited mobility or those living in remote and inaccessible areas.

Moreover, electronic democracy can contribute to the broader participation of citizens from various social and economic strata of society. Technologies enable a greater diversity of opinions and represent the interests of all members of society.

The main methods of functioning of electronic democracy include online voting, platforms for exchanging opinions and discussions, and online petitions. The core idea of electronic democracy is to create an open and transparent platform for exchanging information and opinions and providing interaction between society and the government.

However, despite all the advantages of electronic democracy, it also has certain limitations. Data security and confidentiality are among the main problems when developing such systems. Additionally, Internet accessibility may be uneven in various regions of the world, creating obstacles to the full participation of all citizens.

Nevertheless, electronic democracy continues to evolve and become an increasingly common practice worldwide. Many countries already use digital tools to enhance citizen participation and ensure openness and accountability in political processes.

The emergence and development of electronic democracy on the global stage opens up new opportunities for citizen participation in political life and decision-making. However, like any other form of democracy, electronic democracy also faces certain problems and challenges.

The first major problem is Internet accessibility. In developing countries or remote regions, there may be limited or no access to the Internet. This creates inequality in the opportunities for citizens to participate in electronic voting or public consultations. Universal Internet access is required to ensure the successful functioning of electronic democracy.

The second problem is related to data security and the protection of citizens' personal information. When using electronic systems for elections or collecting public opinion, it is crucial to guarantee the security of data transmission and protection against unauthorized access. Otherwise, interference or manipulation of voting results is possible, undermining trust in electronic democracy.

The third problem is the insufficient awareness and technical literacy of the population. For active participation in electronic democracy, citizens need advanced skills in working with computers and the Internet. Without these skills, people are excluded from the decision-making process. Therefore, the successful functioning of electronic democracy requires educational programs to improve the information literacy of the population.

The fourth problem concerns the anonymity and authenticity of participants in the process. In the traditional form of elections, a person's identity is protected by the anonymity of their vote. However, ensuring complete security in electronic systems can be challenging. Moreover, there is a question of the legitimacy of participation in the process only by citizens of a specific state, which also requires special attention and regulation.

The fifth problem is associated with low trust in electronic democracy. Unlike traditional forms of democracy to which people are already accustomed, electronic democracy is a new phenomenon, which raises doubts about its effectiveness and reliability. To increase trust, it is necessary to conduct informational campaigns about the advantages of electronic democracy and its effectiveness.

4. Discussion

There are various forms of electronic participation of citizens in managing state affairs. Electronic voting is one of the essential aspects of electronic democracy, aiming to provide a freer, accessible, and convenient way for citizens to participate in making politically significant decisions. It involves the collection of voters' voices through electronic systems, enabling elections or referendums and a new form of expression of citizens' will within the Russian legal system (the All-Russian Vote) without the need for physical presence at the polling station.

One of the main advantages of electronic voting is its convenience and accessibility. Citizens no longer need to spend time visiting a polling station. They can vote at any time and from anywhere with an Internet connection. This is especially valuable for citizens residing outside their country or those who cannot be physically present due to work or other circumstances.

Moreover, electronic voting can contribute to increased voter turnout. Many people, especially the young and busy, find it challenging to make time to go to a polling station. The option to vote online can make the election participation process more convenient and appealing to such individuals, thereby boosting overall voter turnout.

Electronic voting can also facilitate faster and more accurate election result processing. Traditional methods of vote counting can be time-consuming and susceptible to human errors. In contrast, electronic voting systems make it possible to automatically count votes, minimize the possibility of errors, and deliver results more quickly.

However, electronic voting has several drawbacks that need consideration during its implementation. One of the main disadvantages is the risk of hacking attacks on the system. There is a potential for unauthorized access to voter data or even manipulation of election results through cyber-attacks. This may create uncertainty about the integrity and security of the voting process.

Additionally, electronic voting may pose challenges to the confidentiality of voting. Unlike traditional elections, where voters can express their will anonymously, electronic systems may threaten data privacy. There is a risk of breaching the voter's personal information or leaking their political preferences.

Furthermore, electronic voting may be inaccessible for certain demographic groups. For instance, elderly individuals or those lacking sufficient computer skills or Internet access may encounter difficulties in using electronic voting systems. This could lead to a distortion of election results and create an additional barrier to the participation of such individuals in political life.

In the context of the dynamic digitalization of society, one perspective for developing electronic democracy is its widespread dissemination on a global scale. Currently, various projects and platforms already exist that enable citizens to express their opinions on matters of national importance or make decisions on public forums through the Internet. This opens up new opportunities for broad citizen participation in the country's political life.

A key perspective for the development of electronic democracy lies in the creation of intergovernmental organizations or platforms that bring together countries from around the world for joint decision-making. Such organizations can serve as forums for discussing global issues involving citizens from all countries. This makes it possible to consider diverse interests and perspectives in decision-making.

Another perspective is the development of blockchain technologies, which make it possible to create decentralized governance systems and transparent voting processes. These technologies can ensure data security and prevent the possibility of manipulation of election or referendum results, which could significantly enhance citizens' trust in electronic democracy.

It is also worth noting that electronic democracy can contribute to combating corruption and increasing the transparency of political processes.

After all, thanks to the use of digital technologies, it is possible to create an efficient system for monitoring the expenditure of budgetary funds and detecting instances of corruption. This will help improve the quality of governance and enhance citizens' trust in the authorities.

However, the development of electronic democracy also faces certain obstacles. One of the main problems is the lack of Internet access in some regions or social strata of the population. Consequently, not all citizens can actively participate in electronic voting or express their opinions via the Internet. This creates inequality in participation opportunities and restricts the principles of democracy.

Another issue is protecting citizens' personal data when using e-government and digital platforms for public participation. Laws and technical measures need to be developed to ensure the security of information and prevent data abuse.

Thus, electronic democracy has significant prospects for development on a global scale. It can become a tool for making global decisions, involving citizens in political life, and combating corruption. However, certain obstacles, such as Internet access and personal data protection, must be considered. Developing appropriate technologies and legislation is crucial to the successful advancement of electronic democracy on the world stage.

5. Conclusion

Electronic democracy plays an increasingly significant role in the world. It provides an opportunity for a wide range of people to influence political decisions and contributes to developing an open society. Nevertheless, further research and addressing issues of security, accessibility, and the participation of all layers of society are necessary for the successful implementation of electronic democracy.

Despite the considerable progress that the advent of electronic democracy represents for the development of the political system, it also faces numerous problems and challenges. Active efforts are needed to address these issues by creating an accessible Internet, ensuring data security and protecting citizens' personal information, conducting educational programs to enhance information and legal literacy, and establishing rules and mechanisms to verify the authenticity and anonymity of participants in the process. Only under such conditions can electronic democracy fully realize its potential and become an effective decision-making tool on the global stage.

References

[1] Alekseev, R.A. and Abramov, A.V. Problems and prospects of using electronic voting and blockchain technology in elections in Russia and abroad. Citizen. *Elections. Power.* 1(15): 9–21; 2020.

[2] Arutyunyan, S.A. On the issue of e-government in Russia and foreign countries. *StudNet.* 7: 738–746; 2021.

[3] Avakyan, S.A. The information space of knowledge, digital world and constitutional law. *Constitutional and Municipal Law.* 7: 23–28; 2019.

[4] Belyarov, E.P. Problems of implementation of e-governance and e-government system. *Scientific Journal.* 7(62): 28–29; 2021.

[5] Botnev, V.K. Foreign experience of building e-government. *Sociopolitical Sciences.* 1: 26–28; 2018.

[6] Bronnikov, I.A. Self-organization of citizens in the age of digital communications. *Outlines of Global Transformations: Politics, Economics, Law.* 13(2): 275; 2020.

[7] Gritsenko, E.V. Ensuring basic guarantees of electoral rights in the conditions of informatization of the electoral process. *Constitutional and Municipal Law.* 5: 41–49; 2020.

[8] Kuznetsov, A.A. and Dubinets, E.A. Electronic voting: Problems and prospects of development. *International Journal of Humanities and Natural Sciences.* 4–3(67): 91–95; 2022.

[9] Moskalenko, G.E. Development of electronic democracy in Russia. *Scientific Bulletin of the OMSK Academy of the MIA of Russia.* 1(84): 44–47; 2022.

[10] Musaev, M.M. On the issue of the formation of a modern information society. *Business Bulletin of Entrepreneur.* 5(3): 90–93; 2021.

[11] Nevinsky, V.V. Some issues of legitimization of public power in Russia in the context of the “digitization” of society (to the development of views of Professor V. I. Fadeev). *Courier of Kutafin Moscow State Law University (MSAL).* 9: 123–133; 2019.

[12] Permyakova, A.S, Platonov A.S. and Yumaev E.A. Features of the development of e-democracy in the Russian Federation. Scientific Notes of V.I. *Vernadsky Crimean Federal University. Philosophy. Political science. Culturology.* 5(71): 104–116; 2019.

[13] Pyrma, R.V. The influence of digital communications on political participation. Humanities and Social Sciences. *Bulletin of the Financial University*. 9(4): 63–69; 2019.

[14] Romashkin, T.V. Institutions of the digital economy. *Era of Science*. 15: 65–68; 2018.

[15] Titova, A.I. E-government in Russia and abroad. *Russia: Development Trends and Prospects*. 13–1: 410–415; 2018.

https://doi.org/10.1142/9789811270826_0013

Chapter 13

Implementation of a Service Desk System for Incident Management at a Pharmaceutical Enterprise

Evgeniya A. Sysoeva[†,§], **Ekaterina V. Prutskova**[*,‡,¶] **and Galina V. Arkhipova**[‡,‖]

[†]*National Research Ogarev Mordovia State University, Saransk, Russia*

[‡]*Saransk Cooperative Institute (Branch) of the Russian University of Cooperation, Saransk, Russia*

[§]*e.a.sysoyeva@econom.mrsu.ru*

[¶]*eprutskova@ruc.su*

[‖]*garhipova@ruc.su*

Abstract: This research justifies the need to develop practical recommendations for implementing a service-oriented approach to incident management in the selected pharmaceutical enterprise based on the analysis of its IT infrastructure. The authors revealed that the processes of managing issues and information technologies at the enterprise were being carried out inefficiently. A complete absence of incident recording and systematization was identified, resulting in the regular recurrence of incidents. Additionally, incident reports were often lost due to human

[*]Corresponding author.

factors, significantly increasing the time required for their resolution. The use of a service-oriented approach for organizing the work of the pharmaceutical enterprise's IT service was proposed as a universal solution to the identified problems. The authors study Russian market for incident management information systems of the Service Desk class to implement a Service Desk service within the analyzed enterprise. Based on the Analytic Hierarchy Process (AHP) method, the authors selected the most suitable system for implementation in the pharmaceutical enterprise. Competitive advantages gained by the company from implementing the Service Desk system were considered. The authors concluded that the organization of information processes and IT infrastructure based on the methodology of a service-oriented approach to incident management is currently a necessary condition for ensuring competitiveness for pharmaceutical enterprises and large manufacturing companies in general.

Keywords: Pharmaceutical enterprise; information technology; incident management; service desk system; criterion.

1. Introduction

In the era of shaping the digital economy, information provision has become one of the most crucial areas in company management. The correct and uninterrupted transmission of information is a paramount component of the successful operations of large enterprises, including pharmaceuticals. Special attention should be devoted to the promptness, reliability, and continuity of information processes, which play a significant role in providing data for managerial decisions and contribute to reducing production costs and enhancing operational efficiency.

One of the directions to improve the efficiency of pharmaceutical enterprises is the optimization of their IT infrastructure management. There are various tools for managing IT infrastructure exist, encompassed by the concept of Information Technology Service Management (ITSM) or IT service management. Infrastructure management systems within this model provide a service-oriented approach to the activities of the IT service.

This research aims to study the practice of organizing the IT service at a pharmaceutical ("Biochemist" JSC) and develop practical recommendations for implementing a Service Desk system for incident management in the operations of this economic entity. Achieving the stated goal requires addressing the following tasks:

- To analyze the organizational and economic activities of "Biochemist" JSC.
- To justify the choice of a Service Desk incident management information system using the Analytic Hierarchy Process method for implementation at "Biochemist" JSC.
- To develop a plan for implementing an incident management information system in the pharmaceutical enterprise.

2. Materials and Methods

There are several works by Russian scholars [1–4,7–10] dedicated to researching IT service management tools in enterprises. However, the scientific literature lacks comprehensive studies addressing the implementation of Service Desk systems for incident management in the operations of Russian pharmaceutical enterprises.

The methodological foundation of the research relies on modeling methods, cause-and-effect relationships, and economic–mathematical and analytical methods.

3. Results

The pharmaceutical plant "Biochemist" was founded on November 5, 1959, with the strategic mission of synthesizing antibiotics. In 1987, the plant underwent a reorganization into a Medical Preparations Plant "Biochemist." In 1992, it transformed from a state enterprise into an open JSC "Biochemist." In 2015, it was acquired by the "Promomed" Group of Companies (GC "Promomed") [5]. "Miracle Pharm" LLC, engaged in the wholesale trade of pharmaceutical products, is the founder of "Biochemist" JSC.

"Biochemist" JSC, part of the GC "Promomed," is an enterprise involved in the complete production cycle of medicinal products, from molecule synthesis to the final pharmaceutical form. The plant can manufacture a wide range of medicinal products used in various medical fields, including antiviral drugs and antibiotics to combat infections and medications for endocrinology, neurology, oncology, and general therapy. It houses the largest research center –a complex of laboratories dedicated to developing new drugs and finished pharmaceutical forms. The center's capabilities make it possible to develop new medicinal products, explore and utilize biotechnologies for pharmaceutical purposes, and rapidly scale processes, significantly expediting technology transfer to production and ensuring efficiency growth during debugging and technical launch stages of new medicinal products.

Analysis of the financial performance indicators of "Biochemist" JSC shows that the revenue from the sale of finished goods amounted to 9247 million rubles in 2020, showing an increase of 341.24% compared to 2019 at comparable prices, with a main activity profitability index of 26%, which is 17% higher than in 2019. In 2021, the revenue reached 25610 million rubles, reflecting a 276.97% increase compared to 2020, with a main activity profitability index of 18%, 8% lower than in 2020. In 2022, the revenue amounted to 15031 million rubles, constituting 58.69% of the revenue for 2021; the main activity profitability index was 20%, which is 2% higher than in 2021. Throughout the studied period, the revenue growth rate from product sales amounted to 744.73%; for 2021–2022, it was 58.69%.

The company has contracts with more than 60 leading pharmacy chains, accounting for 75% of the pharmaceutical market in the Russian Federation. The reorganization and modernization initiated in 2015 due to the acquisition by the GC "Promomed" positively impacted the enterprise, resulting in annual production and sales growth of 3–4-fold. Active investment in "Biochemist" JSC, starting in 2020, led to a 13-fold increase in net profit from 2019 to 2022. The enterprise does not plan to reduce its pace. In line with the adopted development strategy for 2022–2026, it will continue the implementation of the reconstruction and technical reequipment program.

The stability of the functioning of information processes in any organization that aims to ensure efficient time and resource management for optimizing its activities and cost reduction is contingent upon its IT infrastructure.

User support at "Biochemist" JSC is handled by the IT department, which receives requests for incident resolution via phone, corporate email, or in-person meetings. However, considering the human factor, a resolution is not guaranteed. The most common user inquiries to the IT department at "Biochemist" JSC include issues with folder access, network unavailability, equipment technical malfunctions, and similar concerns. Additionally, incident recording and systematization are not maintained, leading to the recurrence of the mentioned incidents and other problems within the pharmaceutical enterprise, disrupting the functioning of information processes and impeding or halting information flows.

Given the extensive technical and software infrastructure at "Biochemist" JSC, the absence of incident request systematization, and the high criticality of most IT services (the failure of an IT service immediately halts the company's operations), conditions are created in which the functioning of information processes is cyclically disrupted. The current methods of receiving and storing requests for problem resolution at the enterprise are deemed irrational because many issues remain unresolved for a significant period, limiting the activities of the enterprise's employees during downtime.

The solution to these issues should involve adopting a service-oriented approach to incident management, specifically implementing a Service Desk. One of the main tasks of this service is to address incidents encountered by its users. The Service Desk at "Biochemist" JSC will serve as the point of interaction between the enterprise's employees and IT specialists, ensuring timely, professional, and high-quality resolution of all arising problems. The primary criterion for evaluating the effectiveness of the incident management service's functioning will be the degree of end-user satisfaction.

The primary tasks of the Service Desk include the following:

- Incident and request registration, categorization, and prioritization.
- Problem diagnosis.
- Incident resolution.
- Closure of all authorized incidents, requests, and other inquiries.
- Obtaining user satisfaction feedback upon incident or request closure.
- Informing users in case resolution within agreed-upon timelines is not feasible.
- Communication regarding deadlines for changes and agreed downtime.

Implementing the Incident Management service at "Biochemist" JSC will address issues related to the functioning of information processes, ensuring continuous and effective information exchange. Adherence to the aforementioned system requirements will allow the company to enhance the quality of services and information provided, ultimately positively impacting end-user satisfaction with the Service Desk system, company expenditures on IT infrastructure, and the maintenance of information technologies. Recording and systematizing all requests and incidents will result in standardized solutions for each issue, reducing the downtime of specialists.

Given current trends in adopting a service-oriented approach and maximum automation of all enterprise activities, various versions of Service Desk systems are available on the market. Based on the analysis, four of the most popular and in-demand Russian Service Desk systems have been identified: ITILium, IntraService, vsDesk, and ITSM 365.

The authors identified the following criteria to characterize the considered systems: technical support, compliance with the ITIL model (Information Technology Infrastructure Library), IT asset management, collaboration and personal efficiency, customer support and interaction, knowledge base, security and confidentiality, and other capabilities (Table 1). Performance indicators were defined for the analysis, describing the functional capabilities of the information system and elaborating on the evaluation criteria. This approach makes it possible to assess the chosen information systems comprehensively. For cases where the analyzed indicator aligns with the capabilities of the considered system, a score of "1" is assigned; otherwise, a score of "0" is given. The sum of indicator values forms an overall evaluation for the specified criterion.

Table 1. Characteristics of Service Desk systems.

Criterion	ITILium	IntraService	vsDesk	ITSM 365
Technical support	7.0	10.0	9.0	10.0
ITIL model compliance	7.0	6.0	5.0	7.0
IT asset management	8.0	5.0	1.0	8.0
Collaboration and personal effectiveness	4.0	7.0	6.0	7.0
Customer support and outreach	6.0	9.0	8.0	10.0
Knowledge base	3.0	5.0	2.0	3.0
Security and privacy	0.0	2.0	1.0	2.0
Other capabilities	2.8	6.7	5.6	6.4
Total	37.8	50.7	37.6	53.4

The criteria for selecting information systems and alternatives were pairwise compared, with scores assigned for each criterion. Subsequently, based on the obtained information, the authors formed matrices of pairwise comparisons. Normalization of the matrices was then carried out, determining the weights of criteria and alternative weights. The most significant criteria are "Customer support and interaction" (34.45%), "Compliance with the ITIL model" (19.97%), and "Technical support" (15.19%).

The weight of alternatives is determined based on the incident management system. The most fitting weight for each alternative has been chosen from the standpoint of "Biochemist" JSC. To determine these weights, the authors found the product of the weight matrices of the alternative selection for Service Desk systems and the weights of the criteria for selecting information systems (Table 2).

An essential step in the analysis is assessing the cost of acquiring licenses and the implementation cost for each of the considered Service Desk systems. It is necessary to analyze the price of purchasing shrink-wrap licenses for use on "Biochemist" JSC servers and the cloud-based software delivery model (SaaS solution — Software as a Service). In certain cases, the subscription system may be more advantageous. The cost of each system was calculated using rate calculators and price lists from the developers' solution websites under the following conditions:

- The number of specialists directly involved in processing incoming requests is assumed to be ten.
- The system should provide access to a mobile application for Service Desk system specialists, integrate with 1C (since the information system of "Biochemist" JSC is based on 1C: ERP), telephony, and the Microsoft corporation's directory service for Windows Server operating systems (Active Directory).

Table 2. Matrix of weights of choice alternatives.

Alternatives	Weight (%)
ITILium	16
IntraService	28
vsDesk	10
ITSM 365	45

- For SaaS solutions, a minimum of 300 GB of disk space and one year of extended history storage (system logs and request work histories) are required.
- A deployment support program for the system should be available.

As a result of the analysis of alternatives using the Analytic Hierarchy Process (AHP) method, ITSM 365 [6] is identified as the best Service Desk system for implementation at "Biochemist" JSC. Considering the cost evaluation, implementing the cloud-based ITSM 365 is also a cost-effective solution in terms of the price-to-functionality ratio and it meets all the specified criteria.

The estimated time required to implement the ITSM 365 Service Desk system at "Biochemist" JSC will be approximately 74 hours. Considering a five-day workweek and an 8-hour workday, including lunch breaks and the urgent tasks of IT service specialists, implementing ITSM 365 at the enterprise will take around three weeks.

To determine the economic efficiency of the project, the time spent by an employee on processing a request before the implementation of ITSM 365 was calculated, along with the projected value of this indicator after the introduction of the system. The analysis revealed that using the traditional method, an IT service specialist spends 61 hours per month on request processing. After implementing the ITSM 365 information system, this time will be reduced to 30 hours.

These findings were used to calculate the return on investment (ROI) coefficient. The project is considered profitable if this coefficient is greater than or equal to 100%. In this case, the ROI coefficient was 227.27%, indicating that the investments will be recovered and generate profit. Therefore, the company will receive 2 rubles and 27 kopecks for every invested ruble.

Based on the calculation of the payback period, it was determined that the annual payment for the ITSM 365 system will be recouped in three and a half months. The remaining time will bring a profit amounting to 6,00,000 rubles per year.

4. Discussion

Implementing the ITSM 365 system at the "Biochemist" JSC will make it possible to optimize incident management, ensuring maximum efficiency.

The central element of this optimization will be the ability to register incident requests through various communication channels, including email, telephone, or the personal ITSM 365 cabinet. This will allow the information technology service employees to respond almost instantly to requests, as each specialist will have the ITSM 365 mobile application.

The ITSM 365 system will provide the "Biochemist" JSC with the capability to account for all information technology assets of the enterprise, storing characteristics of each asset, information about owners and the departments where they are utilized, and monitoring the configuration of assets throughout their life cycle.

Implementing the Service Desk system for incident management at the "Biochemist" JSC is necessary for ensuring the pharmaceutical enterprise's competitiveness.

5. Conclusion

This research has demonstrated that the ITSM 365 system enables the automation of change management within the enterprise. The initiator of changes, being an employee of the company, will be able to provide a detailed description of the change, specify the planned date, choose the appropriate category, and select the necessary configuration items. To process change requests efficiently, a member of the IT department will be assigned the role of a system administrator. Fulfilling this role will enable the distribution of change requests among department employees, the setting of priorities, and the approval or rejection of requests. Additionally, IT department employees will be able to add and mark activities necessary for implementing changes, add tasks, coordinate their execution, and conclude incidents.

Automating the incident management process will ensure systematization and order in the IT department's work. Each employee will have a clear understanding of their tasks and the deadlines for their completion.

Managing information processes and IT infrastructure based on implementing the ITSM approach within the company will make the IT infrastructure a reliable and convenient business element. This approach makes it possible to maintain the defined quality of information services, achieve competitive advantages in the core business, and manage profitability.

References

[1] Begicheva, S.V. and Zhukovskaya, I.E. Technical support customer satisfaction research. *Digital Models and Solutions.* 1(2): 35–47; 2022 [cited 2023 September 10]. DOI: 10.29141/2782-4934-2022-1-2-3.

[2] Bogdanova, A.V. Informatization of educational institutions with the application of ITIL principles. *Science Vector of Togliatti State University Series: Economics and Management.* 4(11): 18–20; 2022.

[3] Bogomolov, D.N. and Nesterov, Yu.G. A comparative analysis of ITIL3 and ITIL4. *Trends in the Development of Science and Education.* 72–1: 26–32; 2021 [cited 2023 September 10]. DOI: 10.18411/lj-04-2021-04.

[4] Donskoy, I.S., Budnikova, A.A. and Zamotailova, D.A. IT Service Management using the ITSM Method. In: Popova, E.V. (ed.), *Information Society: Current State and Prospects of Development: Proceedings of the X International Forum. Krasnodar, Russia: Kuban State Agrarian University named after I. T. Trubilin.* pp. 68–70; 2018.

[5] Group of Companies “Promomed.” Official website. [date unknown; cited 2023 September 10]. Available from: https://promomed.ru.

[6] ITSM 365. Official website. [date unknown; cited 2023 September 10]. Available from: https://itsm365.com.

[7] Kulmamirov, S.A., Alymzhanova, Zh.M. and Shametova, G.Q. Comparative review of management systems incidents in IT organizations. *Current Scientific Research in the Modern World.* 2–1(46): 23–30; 2019.

[8] Mikryukov, A.A. and Kuular, A.V. Development of the Incident management model in an enterprise information system based on a three-tier architecture using key (relevant) metrics. *Open Education.* 24(3): 78–86; 2020 June 23 [cited 2023 Sept 10]. DOI: 10.21686/1818-4243-2020-3-78-86.

[9] Slavin, B.B., Neizvestnyy, S.I. and Khudyakov, D.S. Convergence of digital technologies in assessing the efficiency of the processes of the IT departments of the enterprise. *Innovations and Investments.* 4: 267–272; 2023.

[10] Smolyaninova, A.V. Service Desk as an IT service management tool. *Bulletin of Scientific Conferences.* 10–4(62): 135–138; 2020.

https://doi.org/10.1142/9789811270826_0014

Chapter 14

Digital Inclusivity in Sports Training – From High-Performance Sports to Mass Sports

Alexey N. Kokorin[*,†,‡,§], **Kirill P. Bazarin**[†,¶], **Ekaterina V. Nefedova**[†,‖] and **Oksana V. Alexandrova**[†,**]

[†]*Federal Research Center "Krasnoyarsk Science Center of the Siberian Branch of the Russian Academy of Sciences", Krasnoyarsk, Russia*

[‡]*Reshetnev Siberian State University of Science and Technology, Krasnoyarsk, Russia*

[§]*kokorin.an@ksc.krasn.ru*

[¶]*basarin.kp@ksc.krasn.ru*

[‖]*nefedova.ev@ksc.krasn.ru*

[**]*aleksandrova.ov@ksc.krasn.ru*

Abstract: Digital inclusivity in various fields of human activity usually has applications for people with disabilities and other disadvantaged groups. However, when using artificial intelligence in sports, professional athletes are involved in the process, thereby introducing the concept of "digital inclusivity" into mass sports. We have considered the need to create special software for effective support of people in mass

[*]Corresponding author.

sports through the use of artificial intelligence in high-performance sports and the possibility of its adaptation to mass sports. To achieve this objective, we not only conducted a literature review but also interviewed leading experts on individual sports and individuals not engaged in high-performance sports. Based on the results of the literature analysis, we have identified not only breakthrough achievements in the use of artificial intelligence in sports but also problems that do not provide the opportunity to use neural network modeling. Both the literature review and the expert survey have shown that there is significant scope for use of machine learning in almost all sports as well as a large number of well-developed significant parameters for neural network modeling in high-performance sports. Interviews with all groups of respondents have shown that in modern information realities, there is a need to correctly use information for sports training, especially in mass sports, so as to reduce the risk of trauma.

Keywords: Digital inclusivity; artificial intelligence; neural network modeling; machine learning; computer vision; sports; mass sports; physical education.

1. Introduction

The methods of using artificial intelligence (AI) have attracted considerable attention both in the information industry and in society as a whole due to the large amount of information and the possibility of transforming data into useful knowledge and practical solutions. Currently, one of the most discussed topics in the scientific community is the phenomenon of digitalization in conjunction with the use of AI. In various fields, this is even presented as a "great gift," a driver of the transformation of society. The concept of inclusivity literally means "inclusion," and digital inclusivity, in turn, implies the concept that various technologies become available to the majority of interested users.

Digital inclusivity in various fields of human activity is becoming relevant and widely used in the modern world. Digital inclusivity is usually considered in the context of its application to people with disabilities and other minority groups [22,28]. At the present stage of development of modern society and digital technologies, we have reached a level where technologies have significant but mostly untapped potential, and therefore there is a need for their mass application in all areas of our community.

However, the integration of digital inclusivity occurs at different rates in different countries and different types of human activities. The concept of digital inclusivity in the education system has gained the most prominence with the increasing availability of information and communication technologies [3,5]. Recently, there has been rapid progress in the field of AI, which has created unprecedented opportunities for the application of digital inclusivity in various fields of human activity, for example, in economics and, seemingly far from it, in sports – more precisely, not in high-performance sports, in which AI has been used for a long time and successfully, but in mass sports, including physical education [1,2].

The development and maintenance of physical fitness in many countries is an integral part of various national programs. Despite information being available on the correct manner of doing physical education and sports, its correct application depends on many factors. Not only are training methods studied but the physical condition of the athlete himself is also examined, including his physiological and psychological characteristics. Therefore, the transition from the digital profile of an athlete in high-performance sports to digital inclusivity in mass sports requires the creation of extensive databases and, accordingly, specialized software for their analysis and application [4,19].

Not so long ago, AI reached the level required for its use in digital inclusivity in many industries, including sports activity analysis. However, the connection between AI and sports remains unclear both for consumers of this knowledge in sports, who are not well versed in AI issues, and for many experts in the field of AI [1,2,14,18].

At the same time, the introduction of AI into the field of sports has become more widespread. The extensive applicability of neural network modeling algorithms, coupled with the increase in computational power and the accessibility of a multitude of new information sources, has compelled sports federations to explore novel methods for addressing these challenges. All this has brought the use of AI in sports to a new level and has made it more competitive, but the main goal, as before, is to achieve a world-class sports result [10,17].

The following are some areas in which neural network modeling is used most actively [2]:

- game activity/analytics: simulation of match results, player/ball tracking, classification of match events (e.g., throws), referee assistance, and sports betting;

- identification and attraction of talent: selection of athletes, measurement of performance of athletes, and biomechanics;
- training: assessment of the effectiveness of team formation, tactical planning, and modeling of injuries of athletes;
- focus on fans and business: measuring the economic value of an athlete, modeling the demand for event attendance, and optimizing ticket prices.

The goal of digital inclusivity in mass sports, first of all, should be physiological and psychological perceptiveness, and sports results should be based on this. Mass sports with a low probability of injury can be considered a good example for the introduction and analysis of digital inclusivity in sports. On the one hand, mass sports have a good set of specialized hardware and software complexes that allow one to obtain significant information about the technical actions of an athlete, conduct a full set of functional tests during training, and match the results obtained with the results of performances at competitions. On the other hand, mass sports include a wide age range of participants as well as a low risk of injury.

Within the limits of such understanding, the scientific community is particularly interested in analyzing digital inclusivity in sports training. Although there are many methodological and practical solutions for mass sports, the problem of AI application in this field of sports remains open.

There is also a related problem that can and should be considered as an integral part of digital inclusivity in sports training – physical education classes at educational institutions of different levels. A substantial information flow, which captures the attention of students by promising impressive athletic results in a relatively brief period, necessitates that they be able to utilize this information effectively both during and after classes. This is especially true for teenagers who want to develop their sports skills on their own, without paying attention to health safety.

2. Materials and Methods

During the initial analysis of literary sources devoted to the application of digitalization and AI in mass sports, it appeared that there were no serious scientific studies and approaches in this direction. All studies aimed at solving problems in high-performance sports pay little attention to mass sports. Therefore, we are faced with the task of drawing the attention of the scientific community to this problem. We analyzed the necessity, applicability, and continuity of AI methods of high-performance sports for mass sports.

The purpose of our study is to prove the possibility of using AI in mass sports, thereby ensuring digital inclusivity in sports training. In the study, we used the databases of the RSCI, SpringerLink, Google Scholar, Research Information Sharing Service, and Journal Storage. The first 30 records of each database were checked for the use of the following keywords, always associated with phrases such as "in amateur sports," "in mass sports," "in high-performance sports," and "digital inclusivity": AI, computer vision, intelligent text analysis, speech recognition, machine learning, data mining, and visual analytics. When analyzing literary sources, attention was paid to scientific publications over the past 15 years. We identified the use of AI in mass sports according to four methodological criteria: data collection; data processing; modeling and planning of sports training; and user interaction.

In order to learn about the possibility and necessity of using AI in sports practice, we conducted interviews with 18 experts from Russia for each of the following nine sports (i.e., 2 experts from each sport): football, basketball, volleyball, golf, table tennis, judo, athletics, cross-country skiing, and gymnastics. Each of them was an expert in a separate sport with a personal sports career and coaching experience. The interviews were standardized into four different thematic blocks. In the first block, the experts gave an overview of ongoing or implemented projects in the field of AI in sports. This section was used to get an idea of the development of AI in sports. It was based on four previously defined methodological criteria. The interviewees provided us with specific examples of AI use in their sport. The responses to the survey enabled us to categorize the publications dedicated to the problems of AI application in different sports according to the above methodological criteria. This allowed us to determine the number of publications for each criterion. The second block was devoted to the conditions that favor or hinder the successful application of AI in a particular sport. The respondents were asked about the experience of implementing AI in their sports federations, as well as what should be taken into account and what should be avoided. In the third block, we asked the interviewees' opinions about the possibility and necessity of mass practice of their sports by ordinary people of different age groups. The fourth block was devoted to the relevance of the practical implementation of AI in mass sports, taking into account the personal psychophysiological characteristics of people and the risk of injury in different kinds of sports.

To discern the amount of interest shown in the introduction of digital inclusivity in sports training, we interviewed people who are not involved in high-performance sports. The sample included people of different age groups: 16 persons from 14 to 21 years of age, 19 persons from 22 to 29 years of age, 14 persons from 30 to 39 years of age, and 29 persons from 40 years and above. In total, 78 respondents took part in the survey. The interviews were standardized into two different thematic blocks. The first block was devoted to the study of the necessity of practicing non-professional sports. The second, in turn, analyzed the need to use AI during training.

3. Results

The analysis of literary sources revealed 627 publications addressing the issues of the use of AI in sports in general, but at the same time, mass sports became a topic for only 114 publications. The distribution of publications according to the four methodological criteria was as follows: data collection – 181 in sports in general and 28 in mass sports; data processing – 196 and 37, respectively; modeling and planning of sports training – 189 and 36, respectively; and user interaction – 61 and 13, respectively. Thus, data collection, data processing, and modeling and planning of sports training make up the main part of the research of the scientific community, but user interaction, which is required, among other things, for the introduction of digital inclusivity in sports training, only makes up about 10%. A review of scientific publications in the field of computer vision of various sports showed that 41 of the 153 identified literary sources relate to football [8], which is the largest proportion when comparing individual sports [15,16,23]. Publications on hockey [25], basketball [21], and rugby [12] are also illustrative examples. Recently, the number of publications devoted to the practical application of machine learning algorithms has increased dramatically. We found 157 articles on this topic related to high-performance sports and only six articles related to mass sports. Publications can be divided into categories such as forecasting results and analyzing technical and tactical actions. Although forecasting results are of particular interest to the betting industry, technical and tactical analysis is much more attractive to coaches, athletes, and sports scientists because it provides tactical professional recommendations. The means of user interaction occupy the smallest part of the available modern literature, namely, 61 publications on high-performance sports and 13 on mass sports. The issues raised in publications about the use of technologies such as robotics and virtual reality are related to educational goals, rather than improving athletic performance. Similarly, football occupies the largest part of the literature sources found when analyzing a particular sport. When analyzing the use of virtual reality [9], there are 30 scientific papers on various team sports on the use of virtual reality in training. There are also a number of publications that should be paid attention to, which are devoted to basketball [7], handball [27], and rugby [6]. Visual analytics indicates that, for example, the results of machine learning algorithms should not be interpreted incorrectly due to incorrect or incomplete data entered. Visual analytics can automatically analyze and verify the information received, and a person can participate in this process. A brief overview of this problem is presented in the literature [13].

When analyzing the first and second blocks of answers from experts on sports, the literature data confirmed the spread of AI methods in high-performance sports and the presence of problems in all four methodological criteria over the use of AI. According to experts, in some sports, not enough attention is paid to solving problems and full implementation of AI. In general, there is a shift from data collection by means of sensors (the traditional method) to data collection by means of computer vision (based on video). This is mainly due to the fact that data collection should not affect the athlete during training or competition. For example, in contact sports such as judo, as well as gymnastics, athletes cannot use sensors because they negatively affect their performance. Therefore, data collection without wearable devices, for example, using computer vision, is becoming increasingly relevant and plays an important role in the use of AI by athletes and coaches. The interviewees also mentioned examples where spatio-temporal data are collected using computer vision in sports such as football, basketball, and volleyball. In such cases, not only individual athlete profiles are developed, but also a model of tactical team behavior that involves automatic recommendations for the athletes' game actions. Usually, recommendations are not fully taken into account by coaches, but this limitation is based on the fact that coaches need to maintain control over the decision-making process. In individual sports, there are AI algorithms that develop a training plan, but leading athletes are reluctant to follow these plans, which limits the implementation of AI in these sports. Of course, there remain those sports where data collection using wearable devices still plays an important role, for example, in athletics for collecting data on runners to create individual running profiles. Among other things, experts note that the data collection problem is least acute in those sports that have great financial opportunities, such as football or basketball. In general, all experts noted the possibility of using AI in both individual and team sports and cited many parameters that are significant in their sports. When comparing the parameters given by experts with the literature data, we revealed a significant pattern of their use in AI algorithms.

In the third and fourth blocks of expert responses, all of them spoke not only about the possibility but also about the need to promote a healthy lifestyle both through their sports and through mass sports. At the same time, the primary interest was in the massive involvement of children and youth in sports to reveal those with the most talent. Everyone noted the importance of using AI at this stage, as a tool that, on the one hand, will significantly reduce the time and cost for talent search and, on the other hand, will give an informational, economic, and social impetus to a healthy lifestyle and therefore improve the quality of life. In addition, all experts expressed the opinion that the opportunity to receive high-quality information about the training process in each sport, based not only on traditional average training methods but also taking into account the individual characteristics of each person, is a motivating factor for mass sports and will significantly reduce the risk of injury. Another important element that was mentioned by experts is that the idea of using AI should be initiated in the sports community so that the probability of success will be much higher.

A survey of people not involved in high-performance sports showed a 90% general interest in mass sports, while 9% of respondents considered mass sports equal to physical education. The remaining 10% in the age group from 14 to 21 years (2 people), from 30 to 39 years (1 person), and 40 years and above (5 people) expressed an opinion about the uselessness of physical education, especially sports, in their lives. All respondents interested in sports expressed a desire to be able to analyze their psychophysiological characteristics and take them into account when planning training, while six people expressed distrust of the use of AI in the training process. However, if top athletes were to use AI in their training process, these six respondents would also agree to use it.

During the interview, all groups of respondents mentioned interdisciplinarity in the application of AI in sports training, i.e., the presence of representatives from computer science, sports science, and sports in the project, which is consistent with some scientific publications [26]. At the same time, it was noted that the best condition is to have at least one representative in the project who understands all three areas in order to connect all team members. In the scientific world, this is often called the "translation problem."

In addition, the majority of interviewees indicated a need to highlight the issue of digital inclusivity in athletic training within the research, sport, and education communities.

4. Discussion

In most sports, collecting a sufficient volume of information is still an important task. To create an effective AI, it is necessary to collect enough data so that machine learning methods can work correctly. There are two main options for data collection: using wearable devices and using computer vision. Here, first of all, it is necessary to consider in which situations one or the other is generally applicable. Since the use of wearable devices is prohibited in competitions (for example, in football) and in contact sports such as judo, and athletes of sports with high sensitivity (for example, in gymnastics) cannot use sensors, this method simply cannot be used for data collection; therefore, data have to be collected by another applicable method. In general, wearable devices have an advantage in data accuracy, but the main advantage of computer vision is that it does not affect athletes at all.

When combining camera data and data provided by wearable devices, on the condition that the rules do not exclude the use of wearable devices, it is possible to use the position and physical form of several players in team sports. This feature makes it possible to develop and utilize strategies that are difficult for the opponent to counter but well understood by the players themselves. Combining such features and use cases can provide a serious sporting advantage. The combination of several multidirectional sensors will result in even more accurate measurements.

To date, there is a significant gap in data collection in the field of high-performance sports in general. However, in recent years, there has been an information leap in some sports, which has solved the problem of data collection. This should serve as an example, not only for other high-achieving sports but also for mass sports, giving it a nearly ready solution. It should be taken into account that the data situation in sports is not homogeneous at all and cannot be covered by one method. On the one hand, certain large datasets are available, especially in well-funded sports such as football, basketball, and hockey. On the other hand, there are no such large datasets for most other sports, especially non-Olympic ones. This drastically limits the use of neural network modeling techniques in these sports, since large datasets are required for proper AI training.

The use of transfer learning models can come to the rescue in such sports. Models can be trained and validated based on large datasets from related sports and then adjusted. This possibility was mentioned by five experts interviewed in the project. The sport in which they were experts shared basic characteristics with some other sports. A striking example of the use of transfer training is field hockey, although the model was initially trained on football data. By adding other sports that are also compatible in some parameters, such as bandy, to this model, you can achieve a better and more stable result. By highlighting different parameters and transferring them to other sports, the number of related sports will increase significantly, for example, tennis, table tennis, and badminton in terms of racquet sports. Another possibility of applying transfer training may be the dissemination of data from high-performance sports to mass sports, adjusting models for different levels of professionalism and age groups. It is evident that considerations should be given to the issue of data collection about athletes, including their medical profiles, in order to determine the feasibility of techniques that have become established practices for professional athletes but are not widespread in mass sports.

To increase the amount of data received, it is necessary to create communities of experts in the field of AI and sports to expand their knowledge and experience, as well as to introduce representatives from computer science, sports science, and sports, who could become a link for all team members. One of the results of such activities will be access to free and open databases and methods, which will make it possible to easily use them in the development of new reliable AI methods. We call on sports federations to share databases that can serve as a basis not only for the popularization of their sports but also for increasing the number of people involved in mass sports.

When planning an AI project, the availability of modeling methods often depends on the necessary funding as well as the licensed software. In this regard, we propose open-source models and languages [20]. The use of open-source software not only facilitates the financing of projects and increasing their number but also provides the opportunity to involve a larger number of neural network modeling experts in the project, since most experts work exclusively with open-source software.

AI communities are constantly improving their working methods to make them more accessible to students and scientists in the field of sports sciences. If the sports community has a better methodological understanding, it will not only initiate new AI projects in sports but, as we have shown in the results section, it will also increase the chances of success of these projects. The analysis and implementation of AI methods should be utilized not only for large amounts of data but also to develop methods that are designed for smaller amounts of data.

A significant aspect of AI application is how the model is explained and visualized for ordinary participants – not professionals in sports or in AI. This is especially important in mass sports, mainly at the initial stage of training. This approach is the best way for coaches and athletes to validate the utility of the model as well as provide an accurate understanding of the athletic training methodology for a particular sport. In order to increase the accessibility, understanding, and, consequently recognition of AI systems, the visualization of results should always be as informative as possible and easy to read. Methods of dimensionality reduction may be useful in cases when it is required to transfer complex data or optimization results, i.e., the use of generative models.

Virtual and augmented reality can be applied to provide feedback between AI and athletes. Augmented reality can improve the quality of feedback systems in sports. When using virtual and augmented reality models, it is necessary to use real data or data confirmed by subsequent training and competitions. The approximation of such models to various sports should not replace real workouts, but act as athletic learning.

The analysis of literary sources has shown the need to spread AI methods not only in high-performance sports and mass sports but also in physical education classes at school and higher educational institutions. Physical education teachers should have sufficient information and capabilities to conduct physical education classes and provide knowledge about the physical health of students [24]. Previously, physical education teachers had been the main source of knowledge, but today in the era of information dissemination there has been a problem with the correct application of this information, including in sports training. However, the use of AI in education has made it possible to gain individual knowledge and increase the rating of the use of AI [11]. However, when practicing physical education, the use of AI only based on general information about sports training, without taking into account individual characteristics and without the supervision of a coach, can lead to serious problems. Therefore, the development of AI in physical education and mass sports can provide a leap in the quality of life in modern conditions.

In general, since the use of AI in sports is narrowly focused, i.e., mainly aimed at high-performance sports and the digitalization of the same, it gives us reason to believe that the digital inclusivity of sports training should be based on the results of AI in high-performance sports, which should then be adapted to mass sports and physical education classes in educational institutions.

5. Conclusion

Neural network modeling has proved itself not only as a modern tool for data analysis, allowing one to identify complex nonlinear dependencies, the detection of which is difficult by traditional methods of statistical analysis, but also as a methodological approach to the introduction of digital inclusivity in mass sports and physical education. This approach can be used in forming the normative characteristics of athletes, conducting sports selection, developing individual approaches to the organization of the training process, and emphasizing a healthy lifestyle through proper psychophysiological training in mass sports and regular physical exercise throughout a person's life.

Despite the huge number of available literary sources devoted to high-performance sports, there are only a few publications on the use of AI in mass sports. In addition, the introduction of AI at the first stage requires the creation of models of scientific, methodological, and biomedical support for a training system of participants involved in mass sports. This will create the prerequisites for the development of unique software for the effective support of people in mass sports.

In addition to the scientific and methodological approach to the problem of sports training in mass sports, it is necessary to conduct educational activities aimed at instilling the skill of using sports information only from verified sources with mandatory consultation with specialists. In the future, this will make it possible to partially replace the coaching staff in mass sports with AI and adapt people to work with both human and AI assistants, as well as attract additional funding to the problem.

Acknowledgments

The study was conducted with the financial support of the Krasnoyarsk Regional Fund of Science in the context of the scientific project "Development of a regional model of organization of scientific-methodological and medical-biological support of the system of training of the sports reserve of the Krasnoyarsk region on the example of the sport 'Golf'."

References

[1] Bartlett R. Artificial intelligence in sports biomechanics: New dawn or false hope? *Journal of Sports Science and Medicine*. 5: 474–479; 2006.

[2] Beal, R., Norman, T.J. and Ramchurn, S.D. Artificial intelligence for team sports: A survey. *The Knowledge Engineering Review*. 34; 2019. DOI: 10.1017/S0269888919000225.

[3] Brandes, L., Franck, E. and Nuesch, S. Local heroes and superstars: An empirical analysis of star attraction in German soccer. *Journal of Sports Economics*. 9: 266–286; 2008. DOI: 10.1177/1527002507302026.

[4] Chmait, N. Understanding and measuring collective intelligence across different cognitive systems: An information-theoretic approach. *Proceedings of the Twenty-Sixth International Joint Conference on Artificial Intelligence*. Melbourne, Australia: IJCAI; 5171–5172; 2017.

[5] Chmait, N., Westerbeek, H., Eime, R., Robertson, S., Sellitto, C. and Reid, M. Tennis influencers: The player effect on social media engagement and demand for tournament attendance. *Telematics and Informatics*. 50(1): 101381; 2020. DOI: 50:101381.10.1016/j.tele.2020.101381.

[6] Correia, V., Araujo, D., Cummins, A. and Craig, C.M. Perceiving and acting upon spaces in a VR rugby task: Expertise effects in affordance detection and task achievement. *Journal of Sport and Exercise Psychology*. 2012. DOI: 10.1123/jsep.34.3.305.

[7] Covaci, A., Olivier, A.H. and Multon, F. Visual perspective and feedback guidance for VR free-throw training. *IEEE Computer Graphics and Applications*. 35: 55–65; 2015. DOI: 10.1109/MCG.2015.95.

[8] Cust, E.E., Sweeting, A.J., Ball, K. and Robertson, S. Machine and deep learning for sport-specific movement recognition: A systematic review of model development and performance. *Journal of Sports Sciences*. 37: 568–600; 2019. DOI: 10.1080/02640414.2018.1521769.

[9] Faure, C., Limballe, A., Bideau, B. and Kulpa, R. Virtual reality to assess and train team ball sports performance: A scoping review. *Journal of*

Sports Sciences. 38: 192–205; 2020. DOI: 10.1080/02640414.2019.1689807.

[10] Fister, Jr, I., Ljubič, K., Suganthan, P.N., Perc, M. and Fister, I. Computational intelligence in sports: Challenges and opportunities within a new research domain. *Applied Mathematics and Computation*. 262: 178–186; 2015. DOI: 10.1016/j.amc.2015.04.004.

[11] Goksel, N. and Bozkurt, A. (2019). Artificial Intelligence in Education: Current Insights and Future Perspectives. In: Sisman-Ugur, S. and Kurubacak, G. (eds.), *Handbook of Research on Learning in the Age of Transhumanism*. Hershey, PA, USA: IGI Global; pp. 224–236; 2019.

[12] Kapela, R., Swietlicka, A., Rybarczyk, A., Kolanowski, K. and O'Connor, N.E. Real-time event classification in field sport videos. *Signal Process. Image Communication*. 35: 35–45; 2015. DOI: 10.1016/j.image.2015.04.005.

[13] Keim, D.A., Mansmann, F., Schneidewind, J., Thomas, J. and Ziegler, H. (2008). Visual Analytics: Scope and Challenges. In Simoff, S.J., Böhlen, M.H. and Mazeika, A. (eds.), *Visual Data Mining: Theory, Techniques and Tools for Visual Analytics*. Berlin, Heidelberg: Springer; 76–90; 2008. DOI: 10.1007/978-3-540-71080-6_6.

[14] Lapham, A.C. and Bartlett, R.M. The use of artificial intelligence in the analysis of sports performance: A review of applications in human gait analysis and future directions for sports biomechanics. *Journal of Sports Sciences*. 13: 229–237. 1995. DOI: 10.1080/02640419508732232.

[15] Linke, D., Link, D., and Lames, M. Football-specific validity of TRACAB's optical video tracking systems. *PLoS ONE*. 15: e0230179; 2020. DOI: 10.1371/journal.pone.0230179.

[16] Manafifard, M., Ebadi, H. and Abrishami Moghaddam, H. A survey on player tracking in soccer videos. *Computer Vision and Image Understanding*. 159: 19–46; 2017. DOI: 10.1016/j.cviu.2017.02.002.

[17] McCabe, A. and Trevathan, J. Artificial Intelligence in Sports Prediction. In: Latifi, S. (ed.), *Fifth International Conference on Information Technology: New Generations*. Las Vegas, NV: IEEE Computer Society; 1194–1197; 2008. DOI: 10.1109/ITNG.2008.203.

[18] Nadikattu, R.R. Implementation of new ways of artificial intelligence in sports. *Journal of Xidian University*. 14: 5983–5997; 2020. DOI: 10.2139/ssrn.3620017.

[19] Paton, D. and Cooke, A. Attendance at county cricket: An economic analysis. *Journal of Sports Economics*. 6: 24–45: 2005. DOI: 10.1177/1527002503261487.

[20] Pouyanfar, S., Sadiq, S., Yan, Y., Tian, H., Tao, Y. and Reyes, M.P. A survey on deep learning: Algorithms, techniques, and applications. *ACM Computing Surveys*. 51: 1–36; 2018. DOI: 10.1145/3234150.

[21] Ramanathan, V., Huang, J., Abu-El-Haija, S., Gorban, A., Murphy, K. and Fei-Fei, L. Detecting Events and Key Actors in Multi-Person Videos. In: O'Conner, L. (ed.), *IEEE Conference on Computer Vision and Pattern Recognition*. New York, NY: IEEE Computer Society; 3043–3053; 2016. DOI: 10.1109/CVPR.2016.332.

[22] Salas-Pilco, S.Z., Xiao, K. and Oshima, J. Artificial intelligence and new technologies in inclusive education for minority students: A systematic review. *Sustainability*. 14: 13572; 2022. DOI: 10.3390/su142013572.

[23] Stensland, H.K., Gaddam, V.R., Tennoe, M., Helgedagsrud, E., Næss, M. and Alstad H.K. Bagadus: An integrated real-time system for soccer analytics. *ACM Transactions on Multimedia Computing, Communications and Applications*. 10: 1–21; 2014. DOI: 10.1145/2541011.

[24] Tomlinson, S. The irresistible rise of the SEN industry. *Oxford Review of Education*. 38: 267–286; 2012.

[25] Tora, M.R., Chen, J. and Little, J.L. Classification of Puck Possession Events in Ice Hockey. In: O'Conner, L., (ed.), *IEEE Conference on Computer Vision and Pattern Recognition Workshops*. New York, NY: IEEE Computer Society; 147–154; 2017. DOI: 10.1109/CVPRW.2017.24.

[26] Vienni, B. and Simini, F. Interdisciplinarity and global collaboration in biomedical engineering and informatics teaching. *Revista Observatorio*. 4: 486–508; 2018. DOI: 10.20873/uft.2447-4266.2018v4n3p486.

[27] Vignais, N., Kulpa, R., Brault, S., Presse, D. and Bideau, B. Which technology to investigate visual perception in sport: Video vs. virtual reality. *Human Movement Science*. 39: 12–26; 2015. DOI: 10.1016/j.humov.2014.10.006.

[28] You, J.A. Research on Expertise in Teaching. *Korean Journal of Sport Pedagogics*. 7: 41–59; 2000.

https://doi.org/10.1142/9789811270826_0015

Chapter 15

The Utilization of Formal Modeling Languages in the Applied Software of the "Avtopark" System

Ludmila A. Gaynulova[*,†,§], **Alfira M. Akhmedova**[‡,¶], **Irina V. Zhazhneva**[‡,‖], **Guzel Z. Khabibullina**[‡,**] **and Elena Yu. Fadeeva**[‡,††]

[†]*Kazan Cooperative Institute (Branch) of the Russian University of Cooperation, Kazan, Russia*
[‡]*Kazan (Volga Region) Federal University (KFU), Kazan, Russia*
[§]*lagainulova@bk.ru*
[¶]*alfira233@yandex.ru*
[‖]*iraira90@bk.ru*
[**]*hgz1980@rambler.ru*
[††]*lenoktggpy@mail.ru*

Abstract: The digitalization of various sectors of the Russian economy, based on the application of formal modeling languages, is uneven. The development and implementation of applied software in the automotive industry, within the operations of automotive enterprises, pose a pressing issue. This research explores the practical application of formal modeling languages as the foundation for developing specialized systems in

[*]Corresponding author.

the automotive sector. The challenge of accommodating the diversity of initial data in designing the "Avtopark" computer system is addressed as the target domain becomes more focused; the domain's boundaries define the substantive content within it. The formal model being created is thoroughly elaborated upon at every stage of modeling when formal modeling languages are utilized. Another significant argument in favor of choosing formal languages is the correctness of the overall model and its components. For the model implementation of the "Avtopark" system, the authors selected a graph model capable of describing logistics tasks and a network model, where events and tasks constitute the main elements. The implementation of this approach is presented in the form of applied software for the "Avtopark" system, making it possible to implement the majority of existing scenarios for receiving and processing trip orders in real time and allowing automotive enterprises to enhance operational efficiency and substantially reduce costs.

Keywords: Applied software; formal modeling languages; software product; automotive enterprise; scalable digitalization.

1. Introduction

Scalable digitalization, based on the practical application of mathematical modeling, unevenly affects various sectors of the Russian economy. The development and implementation of applied software in the automotive industry, within the operations of automotive enterprises, pose a pressing issue. This research explores the practical application of formal modeling languages, considered the foundation for developing specialized systems in the automotive sector. The authors discuss the characteristic advantages of using formal modeling languages. Adherence to specific conditions and principles of their application makes it possible to evaluate the benefits of such usage. The implementation of this approach is presented in the form of applied software for the "Avtopark" system.

2. Materials and Method

The utilization of digital technologies in the automotive sector has impacted interactions across all levels and in various formats. In the Russian market, the transportation industry employs chatbots, IoT, big data, robotics, OCR, VR/AR, AI, blockchain, and others. The utilization of these technologies in the transportation industry is half as low as the average across Russia. Hence, the issues regarding further digitization of the automotive sector remain relevant. This matter is studied by scholars such as Burdinov *et al.* [1], Georgiev *et al.* [2], Potashev *et al.* [6], Sergeev [7], and Sokolinskaya and Zinovieva [8].

Qualitative advancement toward further transformation of the economy of automotive enterprises through integrating digital technologies is feasible, provided that new requirements for information systems and services are considered. Additionally, it requires the use of advanced computer systems wherein algorithms of actions of all participants in the automotive process are implemented as part of applied software designed to address real-life situations they encounter or may encounter. Consequently, there is a shift in the demands placed on employees of automotive enterprises, necessitating digital competencies and skills. These issues are described by authors such as Georgiev [3], Mardanov and Zhiglij [4], Maslov [5], Stroev [9], and Yefremova and Ignatova [10].

Digitalization of the automotive industry aims to develop and implement comprehensive hardware and software systems to provide a wide range of services in the direction of automotive support for client enterprises. To achieve this goal, two groups of tasks need to be addressed. The first involves analyzing the volumes of goods and services that need to be delivered to clients, considering factors such as delivery time, destination, types of cargo, their weight and dimensions, climatic conditions, and urgency of delivery. The main directions and methods of the second group of tasks will include formulating criteria to optimize delivery routes and calculating transportation costs, considering the financial capabilities of the automotive enterprise. Additionally, it involves the consideration of potential road delays, changes in loading and unloading locations, and flexibility in changing delivery conditions upon client request. The solution to these tasks is presented in the form of applied software for the "Avtopark" system.

Formal languages were used to design the "Avtopark" system software. The problem of considering the variety of initial data in the design of the computer system "Avtopark" is eliminated because the target area becomes narrower. The area's subject content become its boundaries. The developed formal model is thoroughly elaborated at every stage of modeling through formal modeling languages. An important argument in favor of the choice of formal languages is the correctness of the designed model and its particular elements. For the model realization of the "Avtopark" system, the authors chose a graph model, which makes it possible to describe logistics tasks, and a network model, the main elements of which are events and activities.

3. Results

The computer system "Avtopark" is designed to automate a wide range of services aimed at providing automotive support to client companies, including the following:

- Renting vehicles of various capacities for cargo transportation across the entire territory of Russia.
- Organizing transportation routes and calculating optimal delivery schemes to reduce transportation time and save financial resources.
- Providing freight forwarding services, including documentation processing and cargo supervision at all stages of transportation.
- Offering consulting services by competent specialists tailored to the needs of client companies.

Additional options include automating the accounting of comprehensive services for the maintenance and repair of vehicles owned by the automotive enterprise, as well as on-demand vehicle washing and interior cleaning. Furthermore, options for multi-criteria cargo analysis and warehouse activity optimization are available for the automotive enterprise.

The software of the computer system "Avtopark" makes it possible to track services provided to corporate clients comprehensively. This range of services includes providing large-capacity cargo and passenger vehicles, offering seasonal and non-seasonal specialized equipment, and providing services for the technical maintenance and repair of vehicles.

One of the functions of the computer system "Avtopark" is to allocate the required number of vehicles to certain departments. Production necessity dictates, for instance, assigning several business-class and executive-class cars to the management of the automotive enterprise, thus increasing the targeted utilization of vehicles of this level. Similar allocation of vehicles occurs for other structural units of the automotive enterprise. Thus, the goal of the proposed digitalization project for the automotive enterprise is to enhance its operations, achieve process and performance optimization, gain a competitive advantage in its field, and generate additional profit.

The computer system "Avtopark" makes it possible to manage decisions in every specific situation in a timely and judicious manner by recording accurate data regarding the involvement of vehicles of the automotive enterprise in production tasks across different locations. Implementing the computer system "Avtopark" allows the operator of the centralized dispatch center of the automotive enterprise to make optimal decisions in real time regarding the allocation of vehicles for current client demands, ensuring timely control and assistance as needed. Serving as a fleet management system, the computer system "Avtopark" is scalable and suitable for most automotive companies of such a level.

The preparation and implementation of the "Avtopark" computer system initially undergo a trial operation phase. The iterative approach makes it possible to gradually explore the operation of the computer system "Avtopark," transitioning from one stage to another, making it possible to consider all nuances in debugging the system's operation and promptly propose integrating the considered computer system into industrial operation.

Let us characterize the preparation stage. The preparation stage lasts for two to three months. The main objective of this period is to compile a comprehensive technical assignment and coordinate it with the representative of the automotive enterprise. It is necessary to consider the intricacies of the business processes of each structural unit of the automotive enterprise and compile a complete list of requirements and preferences for operating the "Avtopark" computer system. At this stage, all employees of one of the divisions of the automotive enterprise are engaged and tasked with testing the system. These employees of the automotive enterprise must maintain constant communication with the representatives of the working group, promptly and factually inform the members of the working group about the problems encountered in using the "Avtopark" computer system, and fill out all necessary documentation to document and analyze the problems encountered during the debugging process of the system. Thus, a conclusion is drawn regarding the effectiveness of the operation of the computer system "Avtopark"; its viability is evaluated. Concurrently, the technical equipment of the operators' workplaces in the automotive company is verified. Specialists establish internet connections and IP telephony, ensure compliance between the customer's and the executor's systems, and configure access to the operators' workplaces in the "Avtopark" computer system.

Next, it is necessary to characterize the implementation stage. The duration of the implementation stage is two to three months. The primary task of this period is to provide consultations to employees of the automotive enterprise regarding all available options for operating the "Avtopark" computer system. Throughout the implementation stage, the automotive enterprise utilizes the basic functionality of the computer system "Avtopark" on a complimentary basis. During this time, all employees transition to working with the computer system "Avtopark." The system is refined considering the specifics of the automotive enterprise. For instance, it is necessary to address issues concerning the movement of employees within the automotive enterprise's territory, as well as the routes of shuttle buses transporting employees of the automotive enterprise to and from their shifts.

The software of the computer system "Avtopark" ensures data security. Personal protection of employees' personal information is achieved through ordinary algorithms: Unique employee ID numbers are assigned to each employee's surname. Each employee's access to the computer system "Avtopark" is only possible with a personal login and password, making it possible to identify each employee and track the history of orders, system interactions, etc. The computer system "Avtopark" provides options for changing personal data, granting or revoking access rights, or modifying personal data. Anonymization of employees' personal data allows for feedback to be seen in the form of a digital combination. Additionally, there is an option to restrict an employee's access to specific groups of information.

Through the computer system "Avtopark," the unified dispatch center collects information about orders from all divisions of the automotive company. Digitalizing the activities of the automotive enterprise enables dispatchers, when necessary for production needs, to engage in their production tasks from any computerized device in any populated area marked on the map. For this purpose, Internet or Intranet access, as well as a personal login and password, is required.

It is necessary to upload the map of the automotive enterprise's territory into the "Avtopark" computer system and then integrate it with the navigation system. To achieve this, the following steps are required: zoning of the areas through which the enterprise's vehicles move in coordination with the automotive enterprise's management to designate areas for permitted or prohibited vehicle movements. Detailed information about current city addresses and nuances of the automotive landscape should be incorporated into the map. Interactive communication between the map of the automotive enterprise and the computer system "Avtopark" needs to be debugged.

Integration with the navigation module enables the computer system "Avtopark" to form a cartographic navigation complex, incorporating the function of multi-point navigation over a spatially extensive territory of the automotive enterprise. Accurate information regarding warehouse addresses, production territories, and complexes ensures the proper functioning of the computer system "Avtopark" and navigation module. Additionally, it makes it possible to effectively optimize routes and the selection of vehicles with the required key characteristics for the task at hand. When using the computer system "Avtopark," informative standard voice prompts for the driver serve as a convenient addition, covering upcoming changes in the road map, situational route adjustments, as well as comparative characteristics of the permitted speed and the actual speed of the vehicle at any given moment. Furthermore, the voice prompts provide alerts about road markings and the presence of prohibitory signs along the route. An advantageous feature motivating drivers to adhere to work discipline and follow a strictly approved route is the built-in function for recording violations, deviations from the route, etc. Upon recording a violation, the corresponding option, properly configured, notifies the management of the automotive enterprise.

The software of the "Avtopark" computer system makes it possible to generate statistical reports based on necessary criteria in graphical and tabular formats. For instance, vehicle selection criteria may include information such as route, dates and times of travel, distance traveled, and fuel consumption. Typically, driver reports encompass the amount of time spent on the route, the percentage of compliance with traffic rules, and the percentage of adherence to work discipline.

Calculations and practice demonstrate that using the computer system "Avtopark" within the framework of a single automotive enterprise enables the following:

- Completing 50% more trips (requests).
- Selecting a vehicle for a request within five minutes.
- Reducing fleet maintenance expenses by 30%.
- Other benefits.

4. Discussion

This research explores approaches to the practical application of graph and network models in the computer system "Avtopark." It examines the practical use of algorithms associated with these formal mathematical models. The algorithmic solution for the first group of tasks is presented as an approach to representing behavior in the form of a hierarchy of specific processes: finite processes. Each finite process and its place in the hierarchy are described in natural language. The solution to the second group of tasks is based on the concept of a process. A constructed model considers user actions and describes the directive and request–response processes. As a subject of discussion, one can propose the necessity of investigating the effectiveness of using other formal models to solve groups of tasks presented in the second section of the research. Among such models are the intellectual systems model, semantic network model, relational model, and probabilistic model. The implementation of this approach is presented in the form of application software for the computer system "Avtopark," making it possible to realize most existing scenarios for receiving and processing trip orders in real time while also allowing the automotive enterprise to enhance operational efficiency and significantly reduce costs.

5. Conclusion

The research examines the practical application approaches of graph and network models in the computer system "Avtopark." It explores the applied use of algorithms associated with these formal mathematical models. The algorithmic solution to the first group of tasks is presented as an approach to representing behavior in the form of a hierarchy of specific processes: finite processes. Each finite process and its place in the hierarchy are described in natural language. The solution to the second group of tasks is based on the concept of process. The authors constructed a model that considers user actions and describes directive and request–response processes. The implementation of this approach is presented in the form of application software for the computer system "Avtopark."

The software of the computer system "Avtopark," designed to automate the activities of the automotive enterprise, enables the automation of accounting for the provision of the following: rental services for vehicles of various carrying capacities for transporting goods across the entire territory of Russia; organization of transport routes and calculation of optimal delivery schemes to reduce transportation time and save financial resources; provision of cargo forwarding services; consulting services; and comprehensive services for technical maintenance and repair of vehicles. Options for multi-criteria cargo analysis and optimization of warehouse operations of the automotive enterprise are available. The software of the computer system "Avtopark" makes it possible to prepare statistical reports in graphical and tabular formats. For example, a selection of vehicles may include information such as route, dates and times of movements, distance traveled, and amount of fuel consumed. The driver report selection typically includes the amount of time spent on the route, the percentage of compliance with traffic rules, and the percentage of compliance with labor discipline.

References

[1] Burdinov, K.A., Gainulov, E.R. and Karpov, A.I. Synthesis of self-propelled artillery by a video camera mounted on a multicopter UAV. In: Ivanov, D.V. (ed.), *To Scientific Progress – Creativity of the Young: Materials of the International Youth Scientific Conference on Natural and Technical Disciplines*. Yoshkar-Ola, Russia: Volga State University of Technology; pp. 77–79; 2016.

[2] Georgiev, V.O., Biktimirova, K.S., Akhmedova, A.M., Gaynulova, L.A. and Kurmankulova, N.Z. The research on the application of formal mathematical models in industry-oriented development. In: Bogoviz, A.V., Suglobov, A.E., Maloletko, A.N., Kaurova, O.V. and Lobova, S.V. (eds.) *Frontier Information Technology and Systems Research in Cooperative, Economics*. Cham, Switzerland: Springer; pp. 89–97; 2020 September 25 [cited 2023 August 15]. DOI: 10.1007/978-3-030-57831-2_10.

[3] Georgiev, V.O. Software engineering: Technological principles of software development at the level of formalized description, on the example of an abstracted dialog system. *Proceedings of the TEL '2014: International Conference "Language Semantics: Models and Technologies."* pp. 40–41; Kazan, Russia: Fan; 2014.

[4] Mardanov, M.V. and Zhiglij, J.V. The effect of index model rating on the representativeness of the indicators of the quality of the student's education. *Mediterranean Journal of Social Sciences*. 6(3): 714–717; 2015 [cited 2023 August 15]. DOI: 10.5901/mjss.2015.v6n3p714.

[5] Maslov, E.S. Virtualization of logistics functions – an innovative level of management of intelligent transport systems. *Intellect Innovations Investments*.

3: 49–53; 2018 [cited 2023 August 15]. Available from: https://cyberleninka.ru/article/n/virtualizatsiya-logisticheskih-funktsiy-innovatsionnyy-uroven-upravleniya-intellektualnymi-transportnymi-sistemami.

[6] Potashev, A.V., Potasheva, E.V., Ahmedova, A.M. and Gaynulova, L.A. Mathematical modeling of economic processes in the activities of cooperative organizations. In: Bogoviz, A.V., Suglobov, A.E., Maloletko, A.N., Kaurova, O.V. and Lobova, S.V. (eds.), *Frontier Information Technology And Systems Research In Cooperative Economics*. Cham, Switzerland: Springer; pp. 299–308; 2020 September 25 [cited 2023 August 15]. DOI: 10.1007/978-3-030-57831-2_31.

[7] Sergeev, N.A. A brief comparative analysis of the peculiarities of using formal and informal (graphical) modeling languages in designing applied software. *Interexpo GEO-Siberia*. 2005 [cited 2023 August 15]. Available from: https://cyberleninka.ru/article/n/kratkiy-sravnitelnyy-analiz-osobennostey-primeneniya-formalnyh-i-neformalnyh-graficheskih-yazykov-modelirovaniya-v-proektirovanii.

[8] Sokolinskaya, N.E. and Zinovieva, E.A. Key digital future technologies in Russia. *Financial Markets and Banks*. (5): 42–49; 2021 [cited 2023 May 20]. Available from: https://cyberleninka.ru/article/n/klyuchevye-tsifrovye-tehnologii-buduschego-v-rossii.

[9] Stroev, V.V. Development of methodological recommendations for determining the level of effectiveness of measures in the field of digital transformation at knowledge-intensive enterprises. *Bulletin of the Academy of Knowledge*. 49(2): 285–291; 2022 [cited 2023 August 15]. Available from: https://cyberleninka.ru/article/n/razrabotka-metodicheskih-rekomendatsiy-dlya-opredeleniya-urovnya-effektivnosti-provedeniya-meropriyatiy-v-sfere-tsifrovyh.

[10] Yefremova, N.A. and Ignatova, G.V. Some aspects of digitalization of Russian enterprises in current economy. *Vestnik of Saratov State Socio-Economic University*. 3(72): 20–22; 2018 [cited 2023 August 15]. Available from: https://cyberleninka.ru/article/n/osobennosti-tsifrovizatsii-rossiyskih-predpriyatiy-v-sovremennyh-usloviyah.

https://doi.org/10.1142/9789811270826_0016

Chapter 16

Personalization of Sports Activities as a Condition for Improving Quality of Life in the Digitalization Era

Oksana V. Aleksandrova[†,§], **Kirill P. Bazarin**[†,¶] **and Aleksey N. Kokorin**[*,†,‡,‖]

[†]*Federal Research Center Krasnoyarsk Science Center of the Siberian Branch of the Russian Academy of Sciences, Krasnoyarsk, Russia*

[‡]*Reshetnev Siberian State University of Science and Technology, Krasnoyarsk, Russia*

[§]*aleksandrova.ov@ksc.krasn.ru*

[¶]*kpbasarin@gmail.com*

[‖]*kokorin.an@ksc.krasn.ru*

Abstract: This research explains the significance of "psychophysiological data" in sports activities. It demonstrates the potential for transitioning from traditional methods of athletic preparation to personalized methods through the application of artificial intelligence methods. The authors present various methodologies for working with data in sports, employing neural network algorithms to process individual athlete data involving a set of psychophysiological characteristics throughout the

[*]Corresponding author.

stages of preparation. According to the research results, the authors identified barriers to sports accessibility in respondents' perceptions and the reasons for respondents' choice of sports discipline. The methodology of this research is directed toward applied and theoretical aspects. The applied aspects encompass several elements: fostering mass sports participation, establishing digital athlete profiles, optimizing training methodologies for national sports teams and major competitions, establishing a system for nurturing sports talent, and enhancing coaches' qualifications to promote mass sports development. The theoretical aspects include the development of a model for predictive evaluation of sporting success using neural network algorithms, assessing the importance of psychophysiological indicators for athletic performance, and devising a training management model based on individual athlete data. This model adapts flexibly to changes in the athlete's condition to optimize performance outcomes.

Keywords: Digitalization of sport; individualization of sport analytical and psychological support; training process; psychophysiological characteristics; accessibility barriers.

1. Introduction

Digital systems have influenced the fundamental mode of human communication, altered economic and social conditions, and set trends in sports, reshaping directions in athletic activity, for example, the process of selecting specific sports disciplines considering individual characteristics, the organization of training structures, and the efficacy of elite sports. Athletes' clothing and sports equipment can already collect data from their users; there is also software for team management, making it possible to analyze vast amounts of data. This indicates the integration of artificial intelligence technologies into sports and the initial phase of personalizing participants' sporting activities. In sports training and talent selection, AI technologies imply a shift toward personalizing athletic activity as a fundamentally new model of training process management based on individual data and flexibly adapting to changes to achieve optimal results. The digitization of sports activities makes it possible to organize the management of training conditions in mass sports, at the initial stage of talent development and further at the elite level, because it becomes possible to design, plan, and program athletic activities based on the psychophysiological indicators of athletes.

Currently, educational programs aimed at introducing the principles of a healthy lifestyle and health preservation in educational institutions are being developed and implemented within the educational system to attract people to mass sports. By involving the population in mass sports and maintaining an active lifestyle, life expectancy increases and the quality of life improves [7,32,42].

The contemporary sports system consists of two spaces: elite sports, aimed at training top athletes with camps and competitions, and mass sports. Mass sports are designed to develop practical sports skills and readiness to compete (professional success), improve personal development through sports activities, due to psychophysiological characteristics and the type of motivation of those engaged in sports (personal success), and increase involvement in a sports team or sports collective (social success). Creating opportunities for individuals in mass sports leads to the building of a sports activity system in a region. The population of the Krasnoyarsk Territory should have equal opportunities to engage in sports and lead a healthy lifestyle compared to other parts of Russia. Inclusive sports facilitate the fulfillment of individuals' needs to achieve results and success. Sports activities are organized taking into account individual needs and providing the necessary specialized support. Such an approach fosters the gradual growth of widespread participation in sports [25,30–31].

However, barriers to sports accessibility persist in the population's perception, hindering the development of mass sports in Russia and the Krasnoyarsk Territory. Research data related to public perceptions of sports indicate that young people often begin sports activities unconsciously, driven by parental or pedagogical encouragement [7,15,35,47]. People associate "sport" and their personal attitudes toward sports with the following words: "important," "beneficial," "entertaining," "challenging," "difficult," "self-focus, detachment from life problems," "physical and emotional tension," "pleasant bodily fatigue," "rest," "vital necessity," "thrill," "relaxation," "favorite activity," "self-realization," "sports entail hard work," "training requires patience," "positivity," "sports are a way of life norm," "healthy lifestyle," and "not easy at first." Reflecting on emotions associated with stages of engaging in sports, people often describe sequences like "initial enthusiasm, followed by involvement, sustained activity, and eventually burnout..." or "action under control, self-discipline, and creative action…" [7,47]. It is more commonly perceived that sports represent not only a universal right but also a social norm. Among the most preferred sports activities for Russians, football takes the top spot, swimming comes second, and volleyball third; however, Russians also favor walking, athletics (37%), fitness (31%), and strength training (18%). The population perceives "engaging in sports" as involving a structured system and regimen of activities, invariably under the guidance of a professional – a coach or instructor. The barriers to sports accessibility in public perception, which also hinder individuals from incorporating sports into their lifestyles, are as follows: "lack of free time" cited by 46% of people, "desire but not the health" by 39%, "lack of willpower" by 26%, and "lack of funds for individual training sessions with a coach" by 15% [7,32].

The authors selected the sport of golf to explore the barriers to sports accessibility in the perception of the population of the Krasnoyarsk Territory, investigate the reasons for choosing a particular sport, and pilot the application of neural network algorithms to assess the significance of psychophysiological characteristics among novice and elite athletes. The coverage of golfers in the sports reserve training system and the proportion of golfers relative to the total number systemically engaged in golf are very low. There are significant prospects for increasing the popularity of golf in Russia and the Krasnoyarsk Territory, although the value of golf and its benefits for human athletic development are not adequately promoted [4,15,22,25,33,35,47]. Golf is not perceived as a mass sport and is deemed an "exotic" sport due to several reasons: the closed policies of golf clubs, lack of funding for competitions in this sport, insufficient available golf facilities, lack of sports schools, clubs, and sections for children and youth, and insufficient success of Russian golfers in competitions.

To promote golf, it is necessary to develop a methodology for shaping a regional model of sports personalization, serving as a training system for sports reserves and the development of mass sports based on the integration of digital technologies into sports. This research aims to create and pilot a model of effective sports activity based on the consideration of individuals' psychophysiological characteristics, enabling them to successfully engage in golf and monitor their progress in the training process. Through the personalization of sports activities, it will be possible to include a sufficient number of golfers starting from childhood, ensuring the selection of the best and organizing ongoing competitive rivalry among them.

Within the framework of scientific research, the authors analyzed the literature on the issue of personalizing sports activities and the necessity of considering psychophysiological characteristics in sports activities. An evaluation of the significance of these psychophysiological characteristics was provided using neural network algorithms focusing on golf. As part of the research project, the authors conducted case studies of sports organizations in the Krasnoyarsk Territory. The studied organizations test and implement technologies aimed at tracking psychophysiological characteristics. Moreover, they use machine learning algorithms to forecast training results.

The authors chose golf due to its reliance on the psychophysiological aspects of human activity as fundamental and crucial for achievements and successful learning processes. The impact of athletes' physical qualities on golf results, according to expert evaluations, is primarily associated with coordination abilities and vestibular stability, which are paramount for this sport [13–14,19,24,30,45]. Highly skilled players are significantly affected by factors such as warming effect, maintaining consistent performance, and managing psychoemotional arousal and fatigue [17,20–21,23,45]. In sports activities that demand complex coordination and repetitive actions aimed at high-precision targeting (e.g., archery, shooting, and darts), it is particularly important and necessary to consider athletes' psychophysiological characteristics during sports selection and establish individual analytical and psychological support throughout the stages of sports preparation. However, Russian and international scientific publications do not present instrumental studies linking the objective, measurable psychophysiological characteristics of athletes with success in specific sports. Personalizing sports activities represents a promising direction for sports development to enhance opportunities for participation in mass sports, a direction that must be implemented in the region.

In training, athletes seek information on how motor skills are effectively developed in sports activities. Coaches (instructors) must organize communication during sports activities according to the athlete's nervous system type, motivation type, and temperament. The primary task in sports is the necessity of establishing psychological, medical, and analytical support during the training process to effectively develop motor skills in sports activities. Creating databases containing information on the dynamics of skill formation, psychophysiological characteristics, and athlete indicators will enable more efficient achievements in sports activities, adaption to the training process and competitions, and better conditions to engage the population in golf activities [1,5,11–12,34,37,39,41,47].

Personalizing sports activities goes beyond various combinations of nervous system characteristics. It entails factors like preferred sports style, dominant neural activity type, adaptive skills and stability in sporting scenarios, and voluntary self-regulation [5,27,29]. This approach facilitates the systemic organization and qualitative improvement of athletes' sporting activities, aiding in identifying the optimal volume and intensity of training loads [1–2,8–9,18,23,27–28,38,44]. Motivation is a significant aspect that must be considered in personalizing sports activities to maximize its effectiveness in sports achievements [45–47]. To this end, it is necessary to correlate achievement motivation and avoidance of failure motivation with the psychophysiological states and indicators of athletes. Other important aspects of personalizing sports activities include the athlete's individual training style [1,6,10–11,16,18,27,29–30,36,38,45], resilience to monotonous motor skill development activities, monotonous sports activities [2,23,26,40,43–44], extraversion or introversion of the athlete [23,26,40,43], degree of anxiety and rigidity or lability [5,9,27,40], and type of voluntary self-regulation [8,12,15,43,45,46].

For athletes characterized by a melancholic temperament and weakness in nervous processes of excitation and inhibition, the following characteristics are typical and must be considered when organizing sports activities:

(1) **Training method**: It is recommended to use volumetric loads and the volumetric training method, create a state of operational tension during training, and apply a distributed learning system. Lower effectiveness is observed in sports activities during control tasks and competitions; higher effectiveness is observed in training and educational sessions. Athletes of a melancholic temperament with weak nervous processes of excitation and inhibition do not retain motor memory during training breaks due to which sporting skills are poorly preserved. The coach's use of competitive moments in the training process is a factor that creates excessive nervous tension for athletes with a melancholic temperament.
(2) **Motivation**: The athlete's educational motivation influences the effective formation of motor skills during the training process. Educational motivation leads to operational tension caused by the

execution of developing repetitive motor skills. For athletes, the educational motive is most effective. The motive of awaiting assessment of sports activities, such as positive verbal assessment of results and expected future prizes, is less important and ineffective. Negative verbal assessment and reproach of sports activity during skill formation have a negative impact.

(3) **Individual styles**: Athletes with weak nervous processes of excitation and inhibition of a melancholic temperament tend to have a predominant defensive style.

The guidelines for organizing the training and competitive processes of athletes showing pronounced typological characteristics of the nervous system (e.g., inertia or mobility of excitation and inhibition processes, balance or imbalance of nervous system processes), are as follows:

(1) **Training method**: It is recommended to use intensive loads and intensive training methods. Athletes of sanguine and phlegmatic temperaments effectively learn in a state of emotional tension. It is recommended to apply a concentrated learning method in the training process. The regular training environment makes such athletes complacent while competitions stimulate greater effort. Athletes perform extensive training loads and have good motor memory. Phlegmatic temperament athletes with an inert type of nervous system retain motor memory during breaks in the training process, meaning their sporting skills are preserved.

(2) **Motivation**: Athletes of phlegmatic and sanguine temperaments need to experience emotional tension because they require emotional experiences related to discrepancies between expected and actual results, goals, high aspirations, and self-realization in sports activities in order to effectively achieve results. Thus, competitive motivation is significant for them. Achievement motives are necessary for athletes. The expectations regarding the assessment of sports performance are crucial. The motive of negative verbal assessment of sports activities is insignificant and does not affect training effectiveness. The most positive influence for choleric temperament athletes comes from positive verbal assessment by the coach. For such athletes, the educational motive and coach assessment do not impact the effective formation of motor skills and are negative for performance.

(3) **Individual styles**: Each athlete's style is individual (i.e., unique). However, when competing as part of a team, athletes may adopt a combined (i.e., shared, uniform across all team members) style.

2. Materials and Methods

To identify barriers to sports accessibility and the reasons for choosing a particular sport, the authors conducted a survey using golf as an example. A total of 325 individuals participated in the survey, including 69 members of the Golf Association of the Krasnoyarsk Territory and 256 students from universities in the Krasnoyarsk Territory.

The study of psychophysiological characteristics involved 69 members of the Golf Association of the Krasnoyarsk Territory. Two groups were identified: one group consisted of students attending the sports class of the Golf Association of the Krasnoyarsk Territory and the second group included individuals engaged in sports at an amateur level for 1.5–2 years.

The following tools were used to identify the psychophysiological characteristics of athletes:

- "Egoskop," a complex of objective psychological analysis and testing (developed by Medicom MTD LLC, Russian Federation).
- "NS-Psychotest," hardware and software complex (developed by Neurosoft LLC, Russian Federation) [14].
- "ST-150," a stabilometric complex (developed by Mera-TSP LLC, Russian Federation).

Based on neural network algorithms, the authors developed a predictive model for assessing the success of sports activities based on psychophysiological indicators, with an accuracy of approximately 89%, which is significant evidence of the possibility of using neural network algorithms to assess the significance of psychophysiological indicators for golf. The effectiveness of athletic performance depends on psychophysiological indicators and the requirements for athletes' functional preparation. This high level of reliability for athletic performance makes it possible to use neural network algorithms in golf. The authors utilized a fully connected neural network, feedforward architecture, and Python 3.9 development language with the TensorFlow framework for the analysis [1-4,34,39]. The possibility of creating a neural network decision support system was explored.

3. Results

The research involved a survey and interviews with individuals engaged in golf in the Krasnoyarsk Territory to identify barriers to sports accessibility. A total of 325 people participated in the survey, including 69 members of the Golf Association of the Krasnoyarsk Territory and 256 university students from the Krasnoyarsk Territory. Respondents noted that golf is a young and developing sport, which is gaining popularity in Russia. Only 10% of those surveyed were registered in the golf handicap system of the Golf Association in Russia and just 9% visited the live scoring website. Only 3% of respondents were interested in golf competitions and followed news on the Russian Golf Association website.

The survey revealed several barriers to the accessibility of golf in the perception of the population of the Krasnoyarsk Territory: 46% of respondents had only seen golf on the television or in movies, 57% considered golf to be an elite sport, and 68% believed golf was acceptable only for a chosen few. Furthermore, 55% perceived golf as expensive compared to other sports, 62% associated golf with a leisurely pastime for older people, and 85% viewed it as a leisurely and expensive activity.

During the conducted survey, the respondents identified the following reasons for choosing the sport of golf and the advantages associated with personal choice:

- One can master the sport and start playing regardless of age (34% of those surveyed).
- Golf is a youthful sport and holds promise for young people (57%).
- Golf is a visual sport, offering the opportunity to admire nature and landscapes (47%).
- Golf is considered healthier than other sports because training takes place outdoors (86%).
- Golf offers the opportunity for long-distance walking and calorie burning (15%).
- Minimal risk of injury in golf; it is deemed safe (91%).
- Anti-stress effect (68%).

- Golf allows one to focus, meditate, and be active while simultaneously generating positive emotions (75%).
- Golf offers a place for business meetings, decisions, and discussions of business ideas and projects (68%).
- During golf, one has a spontaneous desire to take off one's shoes and slow down to achieve a state of "here and now" (26%).
- Golf opens up new horizons for self-realization (22%).

Considering the specifics of the sport and based on a neural network analysis of the psychophysiological indicators in other sports, the authors compiled a database of the following typological characteristics and informative psychophysiological indicators of individuals engaged in golf:

- Building an individual profile using the tap test based on psychomotor indicators of the nervous system's properties. This is a test to determine the type of nervous system. The test is conducted in two stages. In the first stage, the subject is asked to mark points on a sheet of paper using a pencil with their right hand. In the second stage, they use their left hand. The differences in the number of points marked by different hands in equal time intervals are then determined.
- Attention properties: concentration, stability, and switchability under conditions of active selection of useful information using the Schulte–Platonov table.
- Visual memory and attention volume using the "Remember and Arrange Points" method.
- Determining complex spatial – temporal reactions by testing reactions to a moving object.
- Determining the sensory (latent) period and motor period of simple visual–motor reaction.
- Determining the state of the autonomic nervous system.
- Noise immunity – reaction time with and without interference, interference resistance coefficient.
- Tremorometry – determining changes in hand movement accuracy under the influence of sports activities; measuring tremors to assess the degree of fatigue.
- Vestibulometry – studying the vestibular apparatus and the condition of individual structures of the vestibular analyzer.
- Stabilometry – a quantitative method for assessing balance maintenance functions.

The presented tests can be used to develop comprehensive recommendations for personalizing sports activities, including during the stages of sports selection and the selection of individual programs for individuals engaged in golf.

4. Discussion

As an inclusive resource in the sports system, golf is traditionally viewed as developing coordination abilities (vestibular stability, sense of rhythm, effort modulation, etc.) in people with limited health capabilities. Most researchers examine the correlation between engaging in golf and health, the functional capacity of specific muscle groups, speed–strength abilities, endurance, and flexibility factors. The effectiveness of golf is linked to the stable reproduction of motor skills, coordination, and spatial orientation.

We view inclusiveness as the availability of this sport for the population. Inclusiveness is achieved by identifying and overcoming barriers to access to this sport in people's perception. The goal of ensuring inclusiveness is to popularize golf (i.e., make it widespread) through personalizing athletic activity. Since golf is an individual sport, without contact interaction and unpredictable reactions from opponents altering the overall game space, individual psychophysiological characteristics of the athlete and the coach's (instructor's) actions in organizing sports activities become significant. A golf coach (instructor), armed with diagnostics data of the athlete's psychophysiological characteristics and knowledge of the state of specific motor functions, physical, and coordination abilities, can effectively tailor the athlete's individualization at all stages of sports activity – from initial preparation to the pinnacle of mastery.

5. Conclusion

As a result of this research, the authors identified barriers to golf accessibility in the perception of the population and the factors contributing to golf development in Russia and the Krasnoyarsk Territory, including the establishment of a scientific and methodological support system for sports activities based on digitalization in golf, i.e., the creation of software for digital profiling considering psychophysiological characteristics for amateur and elite athletes and the training of sports reserves. The personalization of sports activities is a significant factor in the mass acceptance and popularization of golf, and a prerequisite for achieving sports results based on forecasting success in the formation of motor skills and leading positions in the global ranking.

This research showed that athletic indicators (e.g., properties of the nervous system, attention switching and volume, visual memory, vision and motor reactions, motor coordination, movement accuracy, and noise tolerance) influence the results and sporting achievements in golf in competitions and during training.

The authors developed a neural network that achieves up to 89% accuracy based on golf. Thus, we can consider it a reliable and significant criterion for assessing the improvement of sports.

Prospects for further research may include detailed experimental studies of athletes' psychophysiological characteristics; the development of training programs considering the specifics of volumetric loads, methods of teaching motor skills, and motivational systems; and the psychophysiological characteristics of sports participants.

Acknowledgments

This research is funded by the Krasnoyarsk Regional Science Foundation within the framework of:

— The project development of a regional model for organizing scientific and methodological provision of the sports reserve training system.
— Medical and biological support for the training system of the sports reserve in the Krasnoyarsk territory, using golf as an example.

References

[1] Government of the Russian Federation. Order No. 3081-r "On approval of the strategy for the development of physical culture and sports in the Russian Federation until 2030". Moscow, Russia; 2020 November 24 [cited 2024 January 26]. Available from: https://docs.cntd.ru/document/566430492?marker=6580IP.

[2] Ministry of Sports of the Russian Federation. Order No. 457 "On approval of the program for the development of golf in the Russian Federation until

2024". Moscow, Russia; 2021 June 22 [cited 2024 January 26]. Available from: https://base.garant.ru/401575768/.

[3] Budnikov, V.S., Semenov A.V. and Bazarin, K.P. Analysis of the significance of psychophysiological markers of athletic giftedness in volleyball using neural network modeling. *Problems of Science.* 5(79): 20–23; 2023 [cited 2024 January 26]. Available from: https://cyberleninka.ru/article/n/analiz-znachimosti-psihofiziologicheskih-markerov-sportivnoy-odarennosti-v-voleybole-s-pomoschyu-neyrosetevogo-modelirovaniya.

[4] Budnikov, V.S., Semenov, A.V. and Bazarin, K.P. Possibilities of neural network analysis of psychophysiological markers of athletic giftedness in volleyball. *Problems of Science.* 5(79): 29–31; 2023 [cited 2024 January 26]. Available from: https://cyberleninka.ru/article/n/vozmozhnosti-neyrosetevogo-analiza-psihofiziologicheskih-markerov-sportivnoy-odarennosti-v-voleybole.

[5] Chebin, V.G. (ed.), Student golf in Russia: Current state and prospects: Materials of the All-Russian Scientific and Practical Conference [Internet]. St. Petersburg, Russia: Polytech-Press; 2020 November 20 [cited 2024 January 20]. Available from: https://ifkst.spbstu.ru/userfiles/files/konferenchiya/SBORNIK-STUDENCHESKIY-GOLF-ROSSII-2020.pdf.

[6] Eganov, A.V. and Sirotin, O.A. Technology for developing a methodology for evaluating the competitive performance of high-skill judoka. *Russian Journal of Physical education and sport.* 3(28): 41–49; 2013 [cited 2024 January 26]. Available from: https://cyberleninka.ru/article/n/tehnologiya-razrabotki-metodiki-otsenki-sorevnovatelnoy-deyatelnosti-dzyudoistov-vysokoy-kvalifikatsii.pdf.

[7] Fetiskin, N.P. A systemic study of monotony in professional activity (Synopsis of Dissertation of Doctor of Psychological Sciences). St. Petersburg, Russia: St. Petersburg University; 1993.

[8] Gritsayenko, M.V. and Romanina, E.V. Psychological peculiarities of competitive activity of shooting athletes. In: *Current Trends and Problems of Development of Physical Culture, Sport and Tourism in Society*. Voronezh; Russia; pp. 14–16; 2000.

[9] Ilyin, E.P. Psychology of sport. St. Petersburg, Russia: Piter; pp. 200–223; 2008.

[10] Ilyin, E.P., Kiselev, Yu,Ya. and Safonov, V.K. Psychology of sport. *Modern Directions of Psychological Science: Textbook.* Leningrad, USSR: Leningrad State University; p. 56–78; 1989.

[11] Kalmykov, E.V. *Individualization of Tactical Training of Boxers in Relation to the Peculiarities of Psychological Qualities Affecting Tactical Skills*, Synopsis of Dissertation of Candidate of Pedagogical Studies. Moscow, USSR: GTSOLIFK; 1982.

[12] Klimov, E.A. *Individual Style of Activity Depending on Typological Properties of Nervous System: To Psychological Bases of Organization of*

Work, Teaching, Sports, (Synopsis of Dissertation of Doctor of Psychological Studies). Kazan, Russia: Kazan University; 1969.

[13] Kofman, L.B. and Kurashvili, V.A. Innovative methods of psychophysiological analysis of athletes' performance. *Sports Science Bulletin*. 3: 19–23; 2015.

[14] Korolkov, A.N. and Langueva, O.V. and Lysov, E.A. Assessment of general patterns of competitive results change in sports mini-golf. *Scientific Notes of Lesgaft University*. 2(204): 242–247; 2022.

[15] Korolkov, A.N. and Verchenov, V.V. The content of multi-year training of young golfers. *Voronezh, Russia: Scientific Book*. pp. 325–400; 2014.

[16] Korolkov, A.N. and Zherebko, D.S. Factors determining the position of golfers in the world ranking. *Theory and Practice of Physical Culture*. 2: 53–55; 2013.

[17] Korolkov, A.N. *Content of Sports Training in Golf: Textbook*. Moscow, Russia: Editus; pp. 85–152; 2016.

[18] Korolkov, A.N. *Physical Fitness in Golf*. Saarbrücken, Germany: LAP Lambert; pp. 98–160; 2013.

[19] Korolkov, A.N. Tactical and technical training and analysis of competitive performance in golf and mini-golf. In: *Traditions And Innovations in The System of Training Athletes and Sports Personnel: Materials of the I All-Russian Branch Scientific Internet Conference of Teachers of Sports Universities in Online Mode*. Moscow, Russia: Russian State University of Physical Education, Sport, Youth and Tourism "RSUPESY&T"; pp. 81–85; 2013.

[20] Korolkov, A.N. Trends in sports excellence in golf based on the results of the Russian championships 2012–2022. *Scientific Notes of Lesgaft University*. 1: 253–258; 2023.

[21] Mantrova, I.N. *Methodological Guide to Psychophysiological and Psychological Diagnostics*. Ivanovo, Russia: Neurosoft; 2007.

[22] McGimpsey, K. and Neech, D. In: Grebnev, M. Translation from English; Nikolov A. (ed.), *Golf: Implements and Memorabilia*. Moscow, Russia: Publishing House "Anatolia"; pp. 55–89; 2006.

[23] Merlin, V.S. *An Outline of the Integral Study of Individuality*. Moscow, USSR: Prosveshhenie; pp. 158–207; 1986.

[24] Merlinkin, V.P. Typological features of initial skill formation of acrobatic athletes. In: *Psychological Issues of Training and Athlete Readiness for Competition*. Moscow, USSR: Physical Education and Sport; pp. 187–191: 1969.

[25] Morosanova, V.I. *Individual Self-Regulation Style: Phenomenon, Structure and Functions in Human Voluntary Activity*. Moscow, Russia: Nauka; pp. 56–79; 1998.

[26] Murray, A.D., Daines, L., Archibald, D., Hawkes, R.A., Schiphorst, C., Kelly, P., *et al.* The relationships between golf and health: A scoping review. *Review. British Journal of Sports Medicine*. 51: 12–19; 2016 [cited 2024 January 25]. DOI: 10.1136/bjsports-2016-096625.

[27] Nikiforov, V.E. Methods and means of studying the psychological structure of sports activity. *Theory and Practice of Physical Culture*. 7: 9–12; 1978.

[28] Popov, A.L. *Sports Psychology: Textbook*. 4th edn. Moscow, Russia: Moscow Psychological and Social Institute; Flinta; pp. 68–92; 2013.

[29] Potoroka, G.G. *Initial Training of Technical-Tactical Actions in Judo Taking into Account the Properties of the Nervous System and Temperament of Students,* Synopsis of Dissertation of Candidate of Pedagogical Sciences. Leningrad, USSR: Leningrad Institute of Physical Education "GTSOLIFK"; 1986.

[30] Rakhmatov, A.I., Mashoshina, I.V., Germanov, G.N. and Korolkov, A.N. Sports and spectacular forms of national games in technologies of the organization of motive activity of school students. *Physical Culture and Health*. 56(1): 101–106; 2016.

[31] Ridpath, B.D. *Alternative Models of Sport Development in America: Solutions to a Crisis in Education and Public Health Paperback*, 1st edn. Athens, OH: Ohio University Press; 2018.

[32] Rodionov, A.V. and Khudadov, N.A. Psychological aspects of training high-level athletes. In: Rudik, P.A., Medvedev, B.B. and Rodionov, A.V. (eds.), *Psychology and Modern Sport: International Collection of Scientific Works*. Moscow, USSR: Physical education and sport; pp. 103–112; 1982.

[33] Rodionov, A.V. Problems of psychology of sport. Theory and Practice of Physical Culture. 6: 2–5; 2006 [cited 2024 January 20]; Available from: http://sportlib.info/Press/TPFK/2006N6/p2-4.htm.

[34] Rozhdestvenskaya, V.I. and Levochkina, I.A. Functional states in monotonous work, and properties of the nervous system. In: Nebylytsyn, V.D. (ed.), *Problems of Differential Psychophysiology*. Moscow, USSR: Pedagogika; pp. 194–222; 1972.

[35] Russian Public Opinion Research Center (VCIOM). Sport for all: Monitoring study. 2023 October 16 [cited 2024 January 25]. Available from: https://wciom.ru/analytical-reviews/analiticheskii-obzor/sport-dlja-vsekh.

[36] Shadrin, V.M. *Psychological Bases of Motor Skill Formation*. Kazan, USSR: Kazan University Publishing House; p. 176; 1978.

[37] Sirotin, O.A. *Psychological and Pedagogical Bases of Individualization of Sports Training of Wrestlers,* Synopsis of Dissertation of Doctor of Pedagogical Sciences. Moscow, Russia: Federal Science Center of Physical Culture and Sport (FSC VNIIFK); 1996.

[38] Smolianov, P., Morrissette, J.N., Ridpath, B.D., Boucher, C., Dion, S., Schoen, C., *et al.* Comparing the practices of US golf against a global model for integrated development of mass and high performance sport. *International Journal of Golf Science*. 9(1); 2020 June 30 [cited 2024 January 25]. Available from: https://www.golfsciencejournal.org/article/13316-comparing-the-practices-of-us-golf-against-a-global-model-for-integrated-development-of-mass-and-high-performance-sport.

[39] Snesar, M.A. and Bazarin, K.P. Development and approbation of the methodology of complex psychophysiological testing for sports selection in the sport "volleyball." *Science, Education, and Culture*. 3(63): 20–23; 2022.

[40] Snesar, M.A. and Bazarin, K.P. Psychophysiological markers of athletic giftedness in volleyball. *Science, Education, and Culture*. 3(63): 45–47; 2022.

[41] Sopov, V.F. *Mental States in Stressful Professional Activities*. Moscow, Russia: Academic project; pp. 99–127; 2020.

[42] Sopov, V.F. *Theory and Methodology of Psychological Training in Modern Sport: Methodical Manual*. Moscow, Russia: ICLC; pp. 68–119; 2010.

[43] Striano, P. *Anatomy, Stretching & Training for Golfers*. New York, NY: Skyhorse Publishing. p. 160; 2014.

[44] Tolochek, V.A. The problem of individual activity style in psychology: Past, present and future. *Bulletin of Moscow University, Psychology*. 2: 43–51; 2010.

[45] Vorontsov, V.V. Manifestation of individual and typological personal peculiarities within sportive activities. *Siberian Pedagogical Journal*. 5: 373–381; 2010 [cited 2024 January 26]. Available from: https://cyberleninka.ru/article/n/proyavlenie-individualno-tipologicheskih-osobennostey-lichnosti-v-sportivnoy-deyatelnosti.

[46] Vyatkin, B.A. *Role of Temperament in Sports Activity*. Moscow, USSR: Physical Education and Sport; pp. 75–90; 1981.

[47] Zherebko, D.S. and Korolkov, A.N. Accessibility of sports facilities and mass participation in Russian golf. Sport: *Economy, Law, Management*. 1: 35–37; 2015.

https://doi.org/10.1142/9789811270826_bmatter

Conclusion

The digital divide is a relatively new phenomenon caused by the Fourth Industrial Revolution. The information society has yet to fully adapt to the current conditions of the digital divide, while a new wave looms on the horizon due to the anticipated Fifth Industrial Revolution in the coming years. In the era of Industry 4.0, the digital divide mainly pertains to the consumption of digital technologies. In turn, a new manifestation of the digital divide related to employment is likely to emerge in the era of Industry 5.0.

Intelligent machines are actively preparing to become subjects of the information society. Robots, artificial intelligence, machine vision, autonomous transportation, and many other digital technologies are gradually displacing humans from many professions. When the active phase of the Fifth Industrial Revolution begins, the pace of these transformations will significantly accelerate. Differences in labor force participation among members of different social groups may emerge as a probable future manifestation of the digital divide.

The digital divide may manifest in the varying abilities of workers to collaborate with intelligent machines in the workplace. Those workers who are not ready or capable of doing so risk finding themselves outside the labor market. Thus, the Fifth Industrial Revolution may pose new challenges for digital inclusiveness, challenges that entrepreneurial economics 5.0, represented by Industry 5.0 enterprises, can provide powerful and effective responses to.

In this regard, further in-depth exploration of future predictive scenarios of changes in the nature and depth of the digital divide, as well as the capabilities of entrepreneurial economics to ensure digital inclusiveness, should be conducted in continuation of this book. Entrepreneurial economics 5.0 definitely deserves attention as a promising scientific concept in relation to the study of new challenges of digital inclusiveness in light of the impending Fifth Industrial Revolution.

https://doi.org/10.1142/9789811270826_bmatter

Index